Anonymus

Inspector of Reformatory Schools of Ireland

Thirty-Seventh Report

Anonymus

Inspector of Reformatory Schools of Ireland
Thirty-Seventh Report

ISBN/EAN: 9783741197222

Manufactured in Europe, USA, Canada, Australia, Japa

Cover: Foto ©Thomas Meinert / pixelio.de

Manufactured and distributed by brebook publishing software
(www.brebook.com)

Anonymus

Inspector of Reformatory Schools of Ireland

THIRTY-SEVENTH REPORT

OF THE

INSPECTOR

APPOINTED TO VISIT THE

REFORMATORY AND INDUSTRIAL SCHOOLS

OF

IRELAND.

CERTIFIED UNDER THE 21ST AND 22ND VIC., CAP. 103; 31ST AND 32ND VIC., CAP. 59;
AND 31ST VIC., CAP. 25.

Presented to both Houses of Parliament by Command of Her Majesty.

DUBLIN:
PRINTED FOR HER MAJESTY'S STATIONERY OFFICE,
BY ALEXANDER THOM & CO. (LIMITED).

And to be purchased, either directly or through any Bookseller, from
HODGES, FIGGIS, and Co. (LIMITED), 104, Grafton-street, Dublin; or
EYRE and SPOTTISWOODE, East Harding-street, Fleet-street, E.C., and
32, Abingdon-street, Westminster, S.W.; or
JOHN MENZIES & Co., 12, Hanover-street, Edinburgh, and 90, West Nile-street, Glasgow.

1899.

CONTENTS.

THIRTY-SEVENTH REPORT

OF THE

INSPECTOR

OF

REFORMATORY AND INDUSTRIAL SCHOOLS IN IRELAND.

TO THE

RIGHT HON. GERALD W. BALFOUR, P.C., M.P.,

&c., &c.,

CHIEF SECRETARY TO THE LORD LIEUTENANT OF IRELAND.

OFFICE OF INSPECTOR OF REFORMATORY AND
INDUSTRIAL SCHOOLS IN IRELAND,
DUBLIN CASTLE,
25th July, 1899.

SIR,

I have the honour to submit to you the Annual Report on the Reformatory and Industrial Schools in Ireland, for the year ending 31st December, 1898.

During that year there were under inspection 6 Reformatory and 71 Industrial Schools.

REFORMATORIES.

There are 6 Reformatory Schools in Ireland—

2 for Roman Catholic Boys.
3 „ „ Girls.
1 for Protestant Boys.

The 2 schools for Roman Catholic boys are situated at Philipstown, in King's County, and Glencree, County Wicklow, and had under detention respectively at the end of the year 208 and 190. The school for Protestant boys, which is situated at Belfast, had under detention 90.

The schools for Roman Catholic girls are situated at Dublin, Limerick, and Monaghan, and had under detention respectively

The following table shows the number of children in these schools on the 81st December, 1807, and on the 31st December, 1806:—

—	On 31st December, 1897.			On 31st December, 1896.		
	Males.	Females.	Total.	Males.	Females.	Total.
In School, ...	510	[illegible]	[illegible]	[illegible]	[illegible]	[illegible]
On Licence, ...	15	1	16	27	2	[illegible]
In Prison, ...	1	-	1	-	-	-
Absconded—sentence unexpired, .	7	-	7	3	-	3
In School—sentence expired, .	-	-	-	-	-	-
Total, ...	[illegible]	[illegible]	[illegible]	[illegible]	46	[illegible]

During the past year 136 were committed to Reformatories It is satisfactory to be able to report that this shows a decrease of 36 in the number as compared with those committed the previous year.

The health of the inmates in both male and female schools was exceptionally good during the year.

From inspection and examination I am satisfied that the literary and industrial training has been well attended to.

The conduct on the whole has been very satisfactory, very few cases of insubordination or absconding having been recorded.

The disposal in the cases of both boys and girls is very gratifying. Boys are encouraged, as far as possible, to qualify for either the Army or Navy, and many of those who have joined the services, have done credit to themselves and the schools.

Financial Statement—Reformatory Schools.

The following table shows the amount received from the Treasury, local rates, other sources, and by industrial profits during the past two years:—

—	1897.	1896.	Increase.	Decrease.
	£ s. d.	£ s. d.	£ s. d.	£ s. d.
Received from Treasury. .	[illegible] 15 3	9,212 17 5	[illegible] 2 2	—
Do. Local Rates. .	[illegible] 10 [illegible]	[illegible] 15 3	[illegible] 4 9	—
Do. Other Sources. .	[illegible] 1 2	[illegible] 19 5	—	7 7 6
Estimated Profit. . . .	[illegible] 10 6	[illegible] 5 8	[illegible] 9 8	—
Total. . . .	[illegible] 6 11	[illegible] 17 4	1,016 15 11	7 7 6

Expenditure.

The following table gives the amounts expended under the same headings for each of the two years ending 31st December 1897 and 1898 :—

—	1897.	1898.	Increase.	Decrease.
	£ s. d.	£ s. d.	£ s. d.	£ s. d.
Salaries of Officers, . .	2,[illegible] [illegible] 2	2,174 9 [illegible]	[illegible] 19 10	—
Rations for do., . .	[illegible]	[illegible]	—	[illegible]
Food for Inmates, . .	[illegible] 16 [illegible]	[illegible]	[illegible] 13 4	—
Clothing for do., . .	1,[illegible] 11 3	1,[illegible] 13 [illegible]	—	[illegible]
Washing, Fuel, Light, . .	[illegible]	[illegible] 17 11	—	[illegible] 11 [illegible]
Repairs, Rates, and Taxes, .	758 [illegible] 7	744 [illegible]	—	13 [illegible] 10
Furniture and Sundries, .	[illegible]	[illegible] 15 [illegible]	—	19 [illegible] 1
Printing, &c., . . .	275 [illegible] 1	[illegible]	[illegible] 1 11	—
Travelling, &c., . . .	[illegible]	[illegible] 14 [illegible]	—	[illegible]
Medical Expenses, . .	[illegible] 18 [illegible]	170 [illegible] 1	[illegible] 1 7	—
Sundries, Rewards, . .	[illegible] 11	546 11 [illegible]	[illegible] 1 10	—
Rent, ...	[illegible]	[illegible]	—	—
Interest, ...	[illegible]	[illegible]	10 [illegible] 11	—
Disposal, ...	467 [illegible] 11	[illegible] 9 11	[illegible]	—
Buildings, ...	[illegible] 16 [illegible]	341 [illegible]	[illegible] 13 [illegible]	—
Loss on Industrial Department,	[illegible] 17 4	—	—	[illegible] 17 4
Total, . .	14,[illegible] 10 [illegible]	14,[illegible] 16 [illegible]	[illegible] 18 1	[illegible] 11 10

The following table shows the cost per head in each Reformatory School for the past two years :—

—	1897.	1898.
	£ s. d.	£ s. d.
Malone, Belfast, ...	21 [illegible]	16 1 10
St. Conleth's, Philipstown, ...	[illegible] 17 10	[illegible] 7
St. Kevin's, Glencree, ...	[illegible] 1 [illegible]	[illegible] 16 7
High Park, Dublin, ...	[illegible] 16 [illegible]	[illegible]
St. Joseph's, Limerick, ...	[illegible] 15 7	[illegible] 7
Spark's Lake, Monaghan, ...	[illegible]	[illegible] 17 [illegible]

St. Conleth's Reformatory for Roman Catholic Boys, Philipstown, King's County.—Average number under detention during

all, without exception, were amenable to discipline, cheerful, happy, and most attentive to their religious duties. Carpentry, shoemaking, tailoring, harness-making, smith-work, baking, gardening, painting, plumbing, and farming are the chief industries in which the boys are engaged, and in all departments they show great aptitude for and love of work. The year 1898 was a record one as regards health. With the exception of one boy who was received in a delicate state, and died notwithstanding the care lavished on him, there was not a serious hospital case during the twelve months.

St. Kevin's Reformatory for Roman Catholic boys, Glencree, Co. Wicklow.—Average number under detention during the year, 181.

The general health of the boys was exceptionally good. The fact that there was no death during the year speaks well for the care bestowed upon the sick and for the sanitary arrangements. The general conduct of the boys was very satisfactory. There were no very serious offences. The boys are docile and cheerful, and during recreation hours enter heartily into the various games provided for them. Carpentry, smith-work, gardening, tailoring, shoemaking, baking, and plumbing are taught. The boys work well at their various trades, and manifest a laudable pride in being able to turn out good and neat work. A number of boys work on the farm, and have many facilities for acquiring a knowledge which will enable them to become hereafter useful farm labourers.

Malone Reformatory for Protestant Boys, Belfast.—Average number under detention during the year, 74.

The boys have enjoyed excellent health. Only one case of absconding occurred during the year, and, on the whole, the general behaviour of the boys has been most satisfactory, and a good tone seems to pervade the school. Carpentry, tailoring, shoemaking, garden and farm work are taught with success. Results have been satisfactory, the percentage of successful cases being most encouraging.

High Park Reformatory for Roman Catholic Girls, Drumcondra, Co. Dublin.—Average number under detention during the year, 28.

With two exceptions, the health of the girls was very good during the year. One girl died of consumption; another, having shown signs of mental derangement, was placed in Richmond Lunatic Asylum, of which Institution she is still an inmate. The children, owing to kind treatment, are bright and happy, and their appearance, after a time, presents a striking contrast to what it was when they first entered the school, utterly neglected as they were. They are well conducted, obedient, contented, and industrious, and a happy homelike spirit prevails amongst them. Needlework of every description is well taught. The girls cut out and make their own clothes. They make kid gloves, and shirts, &c., and supply small orders in other branches of needlework to some of the principal depots in the city. They are taught laundry work, cookery, butter-making, household work poultry rearing, &c. Each girl is trained in that branch of industry for which she shows the greatest aptitude.

St. Joseph's Reformatory for Roman Catholic Girls, Limerick.—Average number under detention during the year, 27.

The health of the inmates has been very satisfactory, as have also been their conduct and discipline. The girls are taught to make and repair their own clothing and outfits. They knit, embroider, upholster, and make Limerick lace. Housekeeping, domestic economy, butter-making, and laundry work are also taught with good results.

Spark's Lake Reformatory for Roman Catholic Girls, Monaghan.—Average number under detention during the year, 8.

The children are taught needlework, and to make and repair their own clothes. They are also instructed in kitchen, dairy, and laundry work. Their health and general conduct during the year have been good.

INDUSTRIAL SCHOOLS.

There were 71 Industrial Schools in Ireland during the year 1898—

17	for Roman Catholic Boys	with certificates for	2,935
44	" " Girls	" "	3,975
4	for Protestant Boys	" "	586
5	" Girls	" "	409
1	Mixed School	for Roman Catholic Girls, 78 and for " Boys, 25	103

The following table gives the number of children under detention in these schools on 31st December, 1897 and 1898:—

Financial Statement—Industrial Schools.

The following table shows the amounts received during the past two years from various sources:—

—	1897.	1898.	Increase.	Decrease.
	£ s. d.	£ s. d.	£ s. d.	£ s. d.
Received from Treasury, .	[illegible] 4 8	101,[illegible] 6 7	1,[illegible] 0 11	—
Do. Local Rates, . .	[illegible] 13 11	41,[illegible] 0 8	1,768 6 4	—
Do. Other Sources, .	9,[illegible] 15 10½	[illegible] 14 6	—	3,[illegible] 1 7½
Estimated Profits, . . .	13,[illegible] 1 8¼	10,373 10 3½	—	[illegible]
Total, . . .	181,143 14 9	[illegible] 16 4½	3,[illegible] 7 3	4,[illegible] 6 7½

Expenditure.

The following table gives the expenditure during the past two years:—

—	1897.	1898.	Increase.	Decrease.
	£ s. d.	£ s. d.	£ s. d.	£ s. d.
Salaries for Officers, . .	17,[illegible] 15 5	17,[illegible] [illegible] 5	19[illegible] [illegible] 0	—
Rations for do., . . .	[illegible] 17 2¼	[illegible]	—	18 19 8¼
Food for Inmates, . . .	62,[illegible] 1 8	62,[illegible] 10 5	64 9 9	—
Clothing for do., . . .	20,[illegible] 15 4	20,151 [illegible] 2¼	—	1[illegible] 19 8¼
Washing, Fuel, Light, . .	18,[illegible] 9 3	18,048 17 10	[illegible] 15 6	—
Repairs, Rates, and Taxes, .	[illegible] 8 2¼	[illegible] 1 6¼	467 18 7	—
Furniture and Sundries, .	[illegible] 19 9	[illegible] 9 6	1[illegible] 0 9	—
Printing, &c., ...	[illegible] 14 7	2,[illegible] 17 8	[illegible] 3 7	—
Travelling, ...	[illegible] 6 3	716 8 7	19 2 4	—
Medical Expenses, . . .	[illegible] 11 6¼	[illegible] 10 3	1[illegible] 18 8¼	—
Sundries, Rewards, . . .	2,[illegible] 8 3	2,816 10 9¼	3 18 0¼	—
Rent, ...	[illegible] 11 4	[illegible] 6 9	33 16 5	—
Interest, ...	[illegible] 4 0	[illegible] 6 0	—	4[illegible] 18 9
Dispensal, ...	3,10[illegible] 9 8¼	[illegible] 14 9	71 4 4½	—
Buildings, ...	[illegible] 12 8¼	[illegible] 8 8¼	—	4,[illegible] 10 8
Loss on Industrial Department.	[illegible] 11 0	[illegible] 16 11	[illegible] 7 8	—
Total, . . .	1[illegible] 1 8¼	1[illegible] 3 6	2,[illegible] 17 7½	4,1[illegible] [illegible] 8

Parental Contribution.

The amount received from this source amounted to £1,021 5s. 8d. as compared with £902 in 1897 and £842 in 1896. This marked increase in the amount is due to the greater energy put into the work by those concerned in the collection.

The law relating to parental contributions towards the support of children in Industrial Schools is most unsatisfactory; it is powerless to compel parents to contribute anything towards the support of their children, and if it were only for the moral effect of making them recognise their parental responsibility, I am of opinion that even the smallest contribution should be rigorously enforced, provided it can be proved that they are able to pay it.

Parental Contribution.

—	Reformatories.	Industrial Schools.	Total.
	£ s. d.	£ s. d.	£ s. d.
Dublin, ...	182 6 8	174 5 1	[illegible]
Provinces, ...	[illegible] 8 7	497 16 5	714 19 10
Total, . . .	[illegible]	[illegible]	1,0[illegible] 5 8

No new schools were established during the year, nor was there any increase granted in the number of children entitled to Treasury payment.

During the year the number discharged, transferred, and died was 1,477. Of this number, 761 were sent to employment or service; 370 returned to friends; 32 emigrated; 18 sent to sea; 3 enlisted; 22 specially discharged; 4 committed to Reformatories; 176 transferred to other schools; 68 died; 5 absconders discharged by expiration of sentence; 18 discharged on account of insufficient grounds for detention. On the whole this is a satisfactory record. Most of the children are well placed, so as to enable them to begin their life work under favourable circumstances.

The question of the discharge and placing out on licence of children, in deference to the requests of parents, is one requiring careful consideration, when submitting such for your decision.

When the home surroundings are morally healthy and the wages of the family fairly good and not precarious, I think it but right that the family tie be restored and parental responsibility re-established. Under such circumstances I have no hesitation in recommending the child for licence or discharge.

In other cases, where I know the home influences are bad or even not good, where the work and the wage are precarious, I hesitate to recommend such for discharge, for I have observed that a child whose habits were but half formed and training imperfect, when sent back to a poor and ill-regulated home, is very likely to drift back into his careless ways and turn out a more mischievous member of society than if he was from the beginning allowed to grow up in the environment to which he had become acclimatised. This has been forcibly illustrated by three cases lately brought under my notice.

I am pleased to be able to report that, on my visits to the Industrial Schools during the year, I found the general tone and management much improved. In a great many schools the improvements I suggested in my last report were in operation; in others, they were about to be adopted; and in all, I found Managers willing to fall in with any suggestion that appeared to them likely to be an advantage to their schools.

There having been a perceptible increase in the committal of a more objectionable class of children than have heretofore found their way to the schools, the question of classification must be taken into consideration. Hitherto there has been no occasion for a change, but now that Managers see a likelihood that children of an objectionable character will be brought forward, they are beginning to demand that special provision should be made for them. They consider that contact with such children would contaminate the simple and pure-minded already in their schools. Such conscientious motives on the part of Managers should be respected, and accommodation should be provided for children considered dangerous to the morals of the well-conducted children in the schools.

This is no new feature in the history of Industrial Schools. In 1881 a school was opened at Kilmore, in the neighbourhood of Artane, to which boys committed under the 13th section might be sent. This was done in deference to the objections raised by Managers to receive them. In 1884, on the occasion of the conversion of St. Joseph's Reformatory School for Roman Catholic Girls, Ballinasloe, to an Industrial School, the then Manager entered into an agreement with the Government to admit all Roman Catholic girls committed under section 13 of the Act from any part of Ireland. In 1880, when Upton Reformatory, was changed to an Industrial School, the Manager specially bound himself to admit to his school all Roman Catholic boys committed under section 13 from any part of Ireland.

In 1894, just thirteen years after its establishment, Kilmore was

From facts like these one must come to the conclusion, either that there are very few children in the country coming within the description in section 13 of the Industrial School Act, or, if they do exist, they are allowed to remain at large.

With regard to the literary and industrial training during the year, I am pleased to say I have noticed a considerable improvement, and a desire on the part of several Managers to adopt views in both branches that are more in harmony with the requirements of recent advances in the system of primary education.

In my last report I had some diffidence in putting forward my views on this subject, and while strongly convinced of their soundness and utility, I had some hesitation in urging their adoption, knowing that they were somewhat at variance with the principles and practice of a system that has been so long in operation in this country. I am pleased to find that what I then advocated in a limited and crude way has now authoritative sanction in the Report recently brought out by the Commissioners on Manual and Practical Instruction in Primary Schools under the Board of National Education in Ireland.

I see no reason why the principles and practices so clearly and cogently advocated in that report should not be adopted in the education of both boys and girls in our Industrial Schools. Managers are not hampered by any hard and fast rules; they have the complete control of their children, and can dispose of their time in whatever way they consider best; while they have exceptional opportunities in such matters as accommodation and appliances, that are wanting in National Schools.

The system I am anxious to introduce, and the merits of which I have discussed with several Managers, is that in which Kindergarten, Manual or Hand and Eye training, and Sloyd are associated with and form part of the school curriculum up to the time the pupil commences technical training in the trade or calling by which he (or she) expects to make a living. Some Managers will not allow that their old-fashioned methods require improvement; others, while constrained to admit the virtues contained in the new Educational Gospel, contend that it would interfere with the time devoted to literary work, and that the change would entail much inconvenience and expense, which they would be slow to undertake.

In the French schools, where Hand-and-Eye training is compulsory, it has been conclusively proved that half the ordinary school time can be given to the training of the hand and eye in elementary schools without lessening the effect of the ordinary instruction, and that, without the training of those organs and bringing them together in their action, we are certainly neglecting that class of culture which to 95 per cent. of the people is of most use to them. "Any work which provides a real training for hand and eye is in the truest sense education."

I have observed when examining Industrial School children that when taken out of the well-beaten track they completely lose their bearing, show little intelligence on the subject-matter in hand, and are painfully deficient in the meaning of words and sentences, and the designation and use of ordinary objects constantly under their observation. As examples of their shortcomings in this regard I may cite a few of the many absurdly amusing answers I got in some of the schools.

In a class of girls—ages from 14 to 16—the word "mail-coach" occurred in a lesson which they were able to read with the greatest fluency. When asked to explain what it was, one said it was "a coach for men"; another said it was a "thrashing machine." Pointing to a gaselier over their heads, I asked what it was. The answers I got were, "gas," "a thing for gas," &c. Asked what they would do in case of an escape of gas into a room, one said she would run for the fire brigade; another for a policeman; another would "turn off the meter." Asked what a meter was, "it was a thing for turning off the gas," "a thing where the gases met," &c.

Most of the girls were well made up in Geography. One was able to tell the source, course, and termination of the Irrawaddy. She was to be a housemaid, and it occurred to me that if she was able to keep a registry of the quantity of gas consumed, and had a practical knowledge of its properties, it would tend more to comfort and security in her future employer's house than any knowledge she possessed about the great rivers of China and Thibet. The system of teaching hitherto followed I hold to be responsible for the state of things I have described; and some Managers, finding that the requirements of the National Board were too exacting and the results disappointing, have already severed their connection with it, in order to be able to devote more time and attention to the education and training of their girls in a manner that will best fit them for the duties they will be called on to perform when they leave their schools. Girls in schools where gas is the illuminant know nothing of the use and care of lamps, and vice versa. I have urged on Managers the necessity there is for giving their girls thorough practical instruction in the nature and use of these every-day requirements, not only with a view of utility, but as a precautionary measure against possible danger. One Manager has told me of a sad case where one of her girls was suffocated by gas in her bedroom a few days after entering on her first engagement as servant. I have urged that in every subject in which Managers profess to teach the children there should be imparted not only a theoretical but a practical knowledge of it, and each child, after being told how to do a thing, should be made to do that thing. I point out that, in the case of training house servants, the knowledge they pick up in doing the ordinary house-work in the school is not sufficient; that they should get a thorough all-round training on all matters pertaining to the duties of general servant, parlour-maid, and house-maid; that a class should be formed for teaching and intelligently performing such commonplace work as boot-polishing, the cleaning and care of silver, the disposal of house refuse, &c., so that we may not hear reports like the following of young servants; one blackleaded her master's tan boots, another commenced her operations on the silver with sandpaper, and a third, thinking that the strainer in the scullery sink was not well adapted for carrying off the rougher *debris*, provided a freer outlet by means of the poker, with the result that the trap got obstructed, and then had to be repaired, after much expenditure in temper and the usual plumber's bill.

I am pleased to be able to report that I have observed a great improvement in regard to some matters to which I drew attention in my last report, and I take this opportunity of acknowledging the beneficial changes that have already been effected in a great many of the schools for girls and are in process of being carried out in others. I should very much like to mention the names of some of these schools that are doing splendid work at the present time, and have further improvements in contemplation, but I refrain from doing so for many reasons. In my next report I hope to substitute for general remarks on the system, a separate report on each school, showing both its excellencies and shortcomings, so that the public may see the character of the work done and the results obtained in each.

To give some idea of the work and how it is done in most of the girls' schools at the present time, I will quote a few extracts from replies I got to queries concerning Kindergarten, cookery, and shopkeeping.

One Manager says:—"Kindergarten makes the little ones fond of school, as it gives variety of occupation, relieves the tedium of ordinary lessons. It keeps both minds and fingers busy, trains their hands and eyes; and the various materials used serve as so many object lessons to open their minds as to form, colour, &c."

Another says:—"Kindergarten has been taught since the school was withdrawn from the National Board. As far as we can judge for the length of time we have been teaching it, it is a most useful subject and has improved the children very much."

Another says:—"I have found and still find the system to be of the greatest benefit to the children. It developes their intellectual and manual faculties, it gives them habits of accuracy and neatness. In a word I must say the Kindergarten, properly taught, has a more favourable effect not alone on the present, but on the after-life of the child."

Against these encomiums the following is the opinion of one of a small number of Managers:—"We have not the Kindergarten in our school. I look on it as a very useless and expensive matter."

On the subject of cookery, one says:—"The technical teacher, Miss M'Curtie, gives regular lessons in cottage cookery. The children are making rapid advances—some are almost experts."

Another says:—A kitchen, such as would be in an ordinary tradesman's house, has been provided, where the girls whose terms expire this year have been trained to prepare the food required for a family."

With reference to shopkeeping, one says:—"Book-keeping and a system of shopkeeping, as recommended by the Inspector, have been taught for the past eighteen months. The children know how to buy and sell, as well as to dispose economically of the wages of an ordinary household. They can keep their accounts neatly and calculate small bills mentally."

Another says:—"A shop has been opened, and the children purchase their weekly necessaries. Manager thinks it will be a great help to the children hereafter, giving them a knowledge of the value of the different articles."

Another says:—"No attempt has been made to teach shopkeeping, as there is no likelihood that any child here will ever be employed in a shop."

Another says:—"Shopkeeping, as recommended in 1898 Report, would not, in my opinion, be of benefit, or compensate for the time it would take up. Such shopkeeping would look like a mere play or sham to these shrewd girls. When possible we send out the elder girls to real shops."

It is not intended that every girl should be a shopkeeper, no more than that every girl who learns to sew or cook should be a dressmaker or cook; but to know the value of money, how to make purchases and keep accounts, as well as to be able to make one's own dress or cook one's own dinner, will very much contribute to the comfort and success of the girls in after life, no matter what may be their calling. A shrewd girl may be a clumsy one, and the practice of tying parcels neatly will give deftness to her fingers; weighing and measuring will tend to accuracy of observation; while the keeping of house accounts will make her apply her theoretical knowledge of arithmetic to a useful practical purpose. I look on the practice as a useful extension of Kindergarten in girls' schools, and one in which the play element is to be commended, while the sham need not render it less educational and instructive.

Kindergarten is now taught in all schools specially set apart for the reception of junior boys. I hope soon to see it established in all the senior schools where young boys are received, and extended into Manual or Hand-and-Eye training, so that the lads may have all their faculties highly educated at the time they usually begin the technical training in the trades or occupations by which they hope to get a living.

I was recently in conversation with the Secretary and the Manager of a large boys' school, when the latter requested that the walls of the yard, where the little lads passed a great part of their time, might be cemented, as they could not be kept from picking out the mortar from between the bricks. I enquired of him if Kindergarten was taught in the school. He said not, and that he knew nothing about it. I explained its object and advantages, with the result that a Kindergarten class is about to be established, when it is to be hoped the youthful energy of the school will expend itself in pursuits of a more educational character than that of picking mortar out of walls.

In two of the large schools for boys that I visited I found classes of from thirty to forty engaged in the monotonous and not highly educational occupation of knitting stockings, under the care of their only councillor and friend, a motherly old woman. This constituted their only Hand-and-Eye training for several hours daily, carried on in most of the cases for several years—in one instance I met a lad who spent six years at this work. The greater portion of their time was devoted to literary studies. There is, I am aware, a strong feeling that the literary training should be kept up to a high standard in our Industrial schools. I am of the same opinion, but I hold it can be done on different lines from those heretofore followed. The teaching of Kindergarten, Manual or Hand-and-Eye training, will not alone not retard the progress in literary knowledge, but will produce just the opposite effect. Bearing on this question the following occurs in the Report on Manual and Practical Instruction already referred to:—

"It is felt that even primary education has a scope wider than the teaching of reading, writing, and arithmetic, or even than the development of the intellectual faculties in general, and that some cultivation of manual dexterity for its own sake may fairly claim to be a proper object of every well ordered system of primary education. It is mentioned, too, by writers of authority, that the cultivation of manual dexterity re-acts advantageously upon the intellectual faculties, and is an important aid to their development."

I hope very soon to see our new Corporate Bodies and County Councils begin to take a more active and practical interest in the Industrial Schools of the county, than was shown by the bodies they replace. The moral disinfection, physical development, and manual and mental education of the poor neglected little waifs of their counties and towns, are surely of as much importance for their consideration, if only from an economic stand point, as are the repairing of roads, planning of sewerage schemes, and carrying out the provisions of the Destructive Insects Act.

With a desire to increase the efficiency of the department, the Lords Commissioners of Her Majesty's Treasury have been pleased to sanction the appointment of an Assistant Inspector, and Mr. C. Graham has been appointed to that office. As regards the general work of the department during the year, I am satisfied that it has been carried on as well as could be expected with the limited staff at my disposal.

I have the honour to be, Sir,

Your obedient Servant,

JOHN FAGAN, F.R.C.S.

APPENDIX.

APPENDIX 1.

Names of Reformatory Schools.

1.—List of Reformatory Schools in Ireland, with date of Certificate, Locality, Name of Corresponding Manager, and Sex and Religion of Young Offenders received.

County.	Name and Situation of Reformatory, Date of Certificate, and Name of Corresponding Manager.
Antrim, . .	1. Malone Reformatory School for Protestant boys, Belfast. Certified 13th March, 1860. Manager, James Lee, Esq.
Dublin, . .	2. High Park Reformatory School for R. C. girls, Drumcondra, Dublin. Certified 21st December, 1858. Manager, Mrs. Mary Tobin.
King's Co., .	3. King's County Reformatory School for R. C. boys, Philipstown. Certified 22nd December, 1870. Manager, Rev. J. Gubbins.
Limerick, . .	4. St. Joseph's Reformatory School for R. C. girls, Limerick. Certified 26th January, 1859. Manager, Mrs. Bridget Haugh.
Monaghan, . .	5. Spark's Lake Reformatory School for R. C. girls, Monaghan. Certified 29th July, 1859. Manager, Mrs. M. X. Finegan.
Wicklow, .	6. St. Kevin's Reformatory School for R. C. boys, Glencree, Enniskerry. Certified 12th April, 1859. Manager, Rev. Patrick Newman.

2.—List of Industrial Schools, showing locality, &c.

County.	Name and Situation of Industrial School, Date of Certificate, and Name of Corresponding Manager.	Number for which Treasury Pay.
Antrim, . .	1. The Ulster Industrial School Training Ship *Grampian*, for Protestant boys, Belfast. Certified 22nd June, 1872. Hon. Secretary, David M'Dowell, esq., Belfast; A. J. O'Rorke, esq., R.N., Capt. Superintendent.	250
" . .	2. Balmoral, Belfast, for young Protestant boys under 10 years of age. Formerly Fox Lodge, which was certified 10th January, 1884. Hon. Sec., David M'Dowell, esq. C.M.—David Barclay, esq.	100
" . .	3. Hampton House Industrial School for Protestant girls, near Belfast. Certified 13th April, 1874. Increased on 5th January, 1897, to 156. C.M.—Rev. A. J. Wilson.	156
" . .	4. St. Patrick's Industrial School for R. C. boys, Milltown, Belfast. This is a transfer of the certificate from the school, Donegall-street, Belfast, certified 27th August, 1869. Re-certified 11th January, 1873. C.M.—Rev. D. M'Cashin, Administrator, Belfast.	150
" . .	*5. St. Patrick's Industrial School for R. C. girls, Belfast. Certified 27th August, 1869. C.M.—Rev. James Hamill, Belfast.	90
" . .	†6. Sacred Heart, Abbeyville, White Abbey, Belfast, for R. C. girls. Certified 5th June, 1896. Increased to 100 on 18th September, 1897. C.M.—Rev. James Hamill.	120
" . .	7. Shamrock Lodge, Belfast, for Protestant Girls. Certified 26th March, 1887. Certificate was increased to 70 on 3rd August, 1892, and again increased to 88 on 8th May, 1895. C.M.—Mrs. Margaret Byers.	88
Armagh, .	8. Middletown Industrial School for R.C. girls. Certified 21st June, 1881. C.M.—Mrs. Mary E. O'Donovan.	50
" . .	9. Lurgan Industrial School for R. C. Girls. Certified 28th April, 1866. C.M.—Mrs. Elizabeth O'Hagan.	50
Cavan, . .	10. St. Joseph's Industrial School for R. C. girls, Cavan. Certified 1st October, 1869. C.M.—Mrs. M. B. M'Kenna.	67
Clare, . .	11. Ennis Industrial School for R. C. girls. Certified 26th February, 1880. C.M.—Mrs. Mary B. Hogan.	80

* The Certificate of St. Patrick's Industrial School for R. C. girls was reduced from [illegible] to 90 on 2nd September, [illegible].

† The Sacred Heart, Abbeyville, Industrial School Certificate was increased from 100 to 120 on 2nd September, [illegible].

2.—LIST OF INDUSTRIAL SCHOOLS—*continued*.

County.	Name and Situation of Industrial School, Date of Certificate, and Name of Corresponding Manager.	Number for which Treasury Pay.
CORK, . .	12. St. Aloysius' Industrial School for R. C. girls, Clonakilty. Certified 13th November, 1869. C.M.—Mrs. M. de S. Murray.	130
" . .	13. St. Coleman's Industrial School for R. C. girls, Queenstown. Certified 5th September, 1870. C.M.—Mrs. Mary B. O'Sullivan.	46
" . .	14. Our Lady of Mercy Industrial School for R. C. girls, Kinsale. Certified 19th November, 1869. C.M.—Mrs. M. E. Fallon.	150
" .	15. Danesfort Industrial School for R. C. boys, Upton, Co. Cork. Certified 13th April, 1889. C.M.—Rev. M. Fennell.	200
" .	16. Cork Industrial School for Protestant boys. Certified on 22nd August, 1892. This school took over the boys who were in the Boys' Home and St. Nicholas' Industrial Schools. C.M.—Edwin Hall, esq.	110
" .	17. Mallow Industrial School for R. C. girls. Certified 10th April, 1880. C.M.—Mrs. M. C Cheevers.	80
" . .	18. The Passage West Industrial School for young boys under 10 years of age, certified 27th September, 1882. C.M.—Mrs. Mary P. Murphy.	60
" .	19. Baltimore Fishing School for R. C. boys. Certified 12th August, 1887. C.M.—Rev. Peter Hill.	150
" . .	20. St. Finbar's Industrial School for R. C. girls, Sunday's Well, Cork. Certified 29th April, 1870. New Buildings re-certified for an increased number of children, 2nd December, 1873. On 27th April, 1897, the Certificate was increased to 173. C.M.—Mrs. Mary Devereux.	173
" .	21. Greenmount Industrial School for R. C. boys. Certified 14th March, 1871. C.M.—Rev. J. R. O'Donoghue.	200
" . .	22. Training Home Industrial School for Protestant girls, Union-quay, a transfer from Glanmire and Passage West schools. Certified 25th October, 1870. Re-certified 14th March, 1871. C.M.—Miss Elizabeth M. Woodroffe. Increased to 60, 13th March, 1896.	60
DONEGAL, .	23. St. Columba, Killybegs, Co. Donegal, for R. C. boys. Certified 20th February, 1896. C.M.—Rev. J. J. O'Donnell.	100

2.—LIST OF INDUSTRIAL SCHOOLS—*continued.*

County.	Name and Situation of Industrial School, Date of Certificate, and Name of Corresponding Manager.	Number for which Treasury Pay.
DUBLIN, . .	24. Artane Industrial School for R. C. boys, Artane. Certified 9th July, 1870. C.M.—Rev. Thomas J. Butler.	800
" . .	25. Booterstown Industrial School for R. C. girls, Booterstown. Certified 10th November, 1870. C.M.—Mrs. K. O'Keefe.	54
" . .	26. Carysfort Industrial School, Blackrock, for R. C. girls. Certified 10th May, 1895.—C.M.—Mrs. Alice Keenan.	80
" . .	27. Golden Bridge Industrial School for R. C. girls. Certified 13th July, 1880. C.M.—Mrs. M. J. Howell.	150
" . .	28. The Carriglea Park Industrial School (formerly Kilmore), Monkstown, co. Dublin, for R. C. boys. Certified 26th September, 1891. Increased to 150 from 1st April, 1896. C.M.—Mr. J. P. Kinahan.	150
" . .	29. St. Mary's Industrial School for R. C. girls, Lakelands, Sandymount. Certified 25th February, 1869. C.M.—Mrs. Frances Mulhall.	70
" . .	30. Meath Industrial School for Protestant boys, Blackrock. Certified 5th May, 1871. C.M.—Robert A. Adderley, esq.	126
" . .	31. Merrion Industrial School for R. C. girls. Certified 10th June, 1872. C.M.—Mrs. Mary Lortaigne.	150
" . .	32. Heytesbury-street Industrial School for Protestant girls, Dublin. Certified 24th July, 1889. Jacob Geoghegan, esq., Hon. Secretary.	55
GALWAY, . .	33. St. Bridget's Industrial School for R. C. girls, Loughrea. Certified 25th November, 1869. C.M.—Mrs. Louisa Smyth.	112
" . .	34. St. Joseph's, Ballinasloe, for R. C. girls. Certified 8th July, 1884. C.M.—Mrs. Mary B. Kelly.	60
" .	35. Clifden Industrial School for R. C. girls, Connemara. Certified 15th July, 1873. C.M.—Mrs. Mary E. Reville.	80
" . .	36. St. Joseph's Industrial School, Letterfrack, Galway, for R. C. boys. Certified 1st April, 1886. C.M.—Rev. T. J. Stephens.	150

2.—List of Industrial Schools—*continued.*

County.	Name and Situation of Industrial School, Date of Certificate, and Name of Corresponding Manager.	Number for which Treasury Pay.
Galway, . .	37. Oughterard Industrial School for R. C. girls. Certified 12th May, 1873. C.M.—Mrs. Elizabeth Martyn.	40
" . .	38. St. Anne's Industrial School for R. C. girls, Galway. Certified 3rd December, 1860. C.M.—Mrs. Mary Leesen.	77
" .	39. Salthill Industrial School for R. C. boys. Certified September, 1871. C.M.—Mr. J. J. Kennedy.	200
Kerry, . .	40. St. Joseph's Home Industrial School, Killarney—For R. C. girls; certified 4th November, 1869. For R. C. young boys; certified 19th August, 1872. C.M.—Mrs. Mary S. B. Irwin.	109
" . .	41. St. Joseph's Industrial School for R. C. boys, Tralee. Certified 25th March, 1871. C.M.—Mr. W. C. Carroll.	100
" .	42. Pembroke Alms House Industrial School for R. C. girls, Tralee. Certified 4th November, 1869. C.M.—Mrs. Mary E. O'Reardon.	70
Kilkenny, .	43. Kilkenny Industrial School for R. C. young boys. Certified 13th December, 1879. C.M.—Mrs. Sarah Byrne.	163
" . .	44. Kilkenny Industrial School for R. C. girls. Certified 22nd March, 1873. C.M.—Mrs. Alicia Beardwood.	100
King's, . .	45. St. John's Industrial School for R. C. girls, Parsonstown. Certified 5th July, 1870. C.M.—Mrs. Mary A. Beckett.	80
Limerick, .	46. St. George's Industrial School for R. C. girls, Limerick. Certified 11th December, 1869. Increased by 20 from 1st April, 1896. C.M.—Mrs. Bridget Haugh.	100
" .	47. St. Vincent's Industrial School for R. C. girls, Limerick. Certified 8th December, 1869. C.M.—Mrs. Mary A. Kenny.	130
" .	48. Limerick School for R. C. boys. Certified 18th August, 1875. Increased to 170, 27th April, 1897. C.M.—Mr. M. M. Brophy.	170
Longford, .	49. Our Lady of Succour Industrial School for R. C. girls, Newtownforbes. Certified 29th November, 1869. C.M.—Mrs. Mary C. Farrington.	145

2.—List of Industrial Schools—*continued.*

County.	Name and Situation of Industrial School, Date of Certificate, and Name of Corresponding Manager.	Number for which Treasury Pay.
Louth, . .	50. House of Charity Industrial School for R. C. boys, Drogheda. Certified 17th October, 1870. C.M.—Mrs. Clare Redman.	92
„ .	51. The Dundalk Industrial School for R. C. girls. Certified 19th July, 1881. C.M.—Mrs. Frances Duffy.	80
Mayo, . .	52. St. Columba Industrial School for R. C. girls, Westport. Certified 13th April, 1871. C.M.—Mrs. M. P. Cullen.	106
„ .	53. St. Francis Xavier's Industrial School for R. C. girls, Ballaghaderreen. Certified 8th June, 1880. C.M.—Mrs. Mary P. Kelly.	75
Monaghan, .	54. St. Martha's Industrial School for R. C. girls, Monaghan. Certified 4th November, 1869. C.M.—Mrs. M. J. Moroney.	67
Roscommon, .	55. St. Monica's Industrial School for R. C. girls, Roscommon. Certified 29th November, 1869. C.M.—Mrs. M. J. O'Beirne.	44
„ .	56. Summerhill Industrial School for R. C. girls, Athlone. Certified 17th October, 1882. C.M.—Mrs. E. Jones.	133
Sligo, . .	57. The Renada Abbey Industrial School for R. C. girls, Tubbercurry. Certified 28th June, 1882. C.M.—Mrs. Bride Fitzgerald.	50
„ .	58. St. Lawrence Industrial School for R. C. girls, Sligo. Certified 22nd April, 1871. C.M.—Mrs. M. T. Neville.	120
Tipperary, .	59. Clonmel Industrial School for R. C. boys. Certified 12th January, 1885. C.M.—Rev. J. Harrington.	150
„ .	60. St. Augustine's Industrial School for R. C. girls, Templemore. Certified 20th August, 1870. C.M.—Mrs. M. R. Crean.	60
„ .	61. St. Francis' Industrial School for R. C. girls, Cashel. Certified 8th December, 1869. C.M.—Mrs. M. Xavier J. Carroll.	110
„ .	62. St. Louis' Industrial School for R. C. girls, Thurles. Certified 11th December, 1869. C.M.—Mrs. M. B. Hogan.	45
„ .	63. Tipperary Industrial School for R. C. girls. Certified 1st May, 1872. C.M.—Mrs. Mary Frances Cantwell.	61

2.—List of Industrial Schools—*continued.*

County.	Name and Situation of Industrial School, Date of Certificate, and Name of Corresponding Manager.	Number for which Treasury Pay.
Tyrone, . .	64. St. Catherine's Industrial School for R. C. girls, Strabane. Certified 30th November, 1869. C.M.—Mrs. Mary Joseph White.	100
Waterford, .	65. Cappoquin Industrial School for R. C. young boys. Certified 1st March, 1873. C.M.—Mrs. M. J. Cullen.	51
" .	66. St. Dominick Industrial School for R. C. girls, Waterford. Certified 13th April, 1871. Was increased to 160 on 27th April, 1897. C.M.—Mrs. Mary A. O'Loughlin.	160
Westmeath, .	67. Mount Carmel Industrial School for R. C. girls, Moate. Certified 9th April, 1870. C.M.—Mrs. M. Bourke.	53
Wexford, .	68. St. Aidan's Industrial School for R. C. girls, New Ross. Certified 13th November, 1869. C.M.—Mrs. Kate Devereux.	70
" .	69. St. Michael's Industrial School for R. C. girls, Wexford. Certified 25th November, 1869. C.M.—Mrs. M. J. Walsh.	106
Wicklow, . .	70. Meath Industrial School for Protestant girls, Bray. Certified 4th October, 1872. C.M.—Mrs. Martha Reddish.	60
" .	71. The Rathdrum Industrial School for young R. C. boys under 10 years of age. Certified 31st December, 1883. C.M.—Mrs. Margt. Tynan.	50
	Totals, . .	7,998

On 31st of December, 1898, there were certificates for —

	Protestant.	Roman Catholic.	Total.
Males, . . .	586	2,925	3,511
Females, . . .	409	3,975	4,384
	995	6,900	7,895
Mixed, ...		103	103
Gross Total, .		7,003	7,998

	Males.	Females.	Mixed.	
Protestant Schools, .	4	5	–	9
Roman Catholic Schools,	17	44	1	62
Total, . .	21	49	1	71

The School at St. Joseph's Home, Killarney, receives both boys and girls—25 of the former and 75 of the latter.

List of PROTESTANT MALE SCHOOLS on 31st December, 1898.

1. The "Grampian,"	250
2. Balmoral,	100
3. Cork Industrial School for Protestant Boys,	110
4. Meath Industrial School, Blackrock,	126
Total,	586

List of PROTESTANT FEMALE SCHOOLS on 31st December, 1898.

1. Hampton House,	156	4. Heytesbury-street,	55
2. Shamrock Lodge,	88	5. Meath, Bray,	50
3. Training Home,	60	Total,	409

List of ROMAN CATHOLIC MALE SCHOOLS on 31st December, 1898.

1. St. Patrick's Male, Milltown,	160	13. Limerick, Male,	170
2. Danesfort, Upton,	200	14. House of Charity, Drogheda,	93
3. Passage, West,	80	15. St. Joseph's, Clonmel,	160
4. Baltimore,	150	16. Cappoquin,	51
5. Greenmount,	200	17. St. Kyran's, Rathdrum,	50
6. Killybegs,	100		
7. Artane,	800	Total,	2,925
8. Carriglea,	130		
9. Letterfrack,	150	*Mixed School.*	
10. Salt Hill, Galway,	200	St. Joseph's Home, Killarney,	25
11. St. Joseph's, Tralee,	100		
12. Kilkenny, Male,	102	Total Roman Catholic Boys,	2,950

List of ROMAN CATHOLIC FEMALE SCHOOLS on 31st December, 1898.

1. St. Patrick's, Female, Crumlin-road,	90	26. St. Vincent's, Limerick,	130
2. Abbeyville,	120	27. Our Lady of Succour, Newtownforbes,	145
3. Middletown,	50	28. St. Joseph's, Dundalk,	80
4. Lurgan,	50	29. St. Columba, Westport,	106
5. Cavan,	87	30. Ballaghaderreen,	75
6. Ennis,	80	31. St. Martha's, Monaghan,	67
7. St. Aloysius, Clonakilty,	130	32. St. Monica's, Roscommon,	44
8. St. Coleman's, Queenstown,	46	33. Summer-hill, Athlone,	133
9. Our Lady of Mercy, Kinsale,	150	34. Benada Abbey, Tubbercurry,	50
10. Mallow,	60	35. St. Laurence, Sligo,	120
11. St. Finbar's, Sunday's Well,	172	36. St. Augustine's, Templemore,	60
12. Booterstown,	54	37. St. Francis', Cashel,	110
13. Carysfort,	80	38. St. Louis', Thurles,	45
14. Golden Bridge,	160	39. Tipperary,	64
15. Lakelands,	70	40. St. Catherine's, Strabane,	100
16. Merrion,	150	41. St. Dominick's, Waterford,	160
17. St. Bridget's, Loughrea,	112	42. Mount Carmel, Moate,	53
18. St. Joseph's, Ballinasloe,	60	43. St. Aidan's, New Ross,	70
19. Clifden, Galway,	80	44. St. Michael's, Wexford,	106
20. Oughterard,	40	Total,	3,975
21. St. Anne's, Galway,	77	*Mixed School.*	
22. Pembroke Alms House, Tralee,	70		
23. Kilkenny, Female,	100	St. Joseph's Home, Killarney,	78
24. St. John's, Parsonstown,	80		
25. St. George's, Limerick,	100	Total Roman Catholic Girls,	4,053

Appendix II.

[illegible]

[illegible]	[illegible]			[illegible]			[illegible]		[illegible]
	[illegible]	[illegible]	[illegible]	[illegible]	[illegible]	[illegible]	[illegible]	[illegible]	
[illegible]	[illegible]	[illegible]	[illegible]	[illegible]	[illegible]	[illegible]	[illegible]	[illegible]	[illegible]
Total.	[illegible]	[illegible]	[illegible]	[illegible]	[illegible]	[illegible]	[illegible]	[illegible]	[illegible]
[illegible]	[illegible]	[illegible]	[illegible]	[illegible]	[illegible]	[illegible]	[illegible]	[illegible]	[illegible]
Total.	[illegible]	[illegible]	[illegible]	[illegible]	[illegible]	[illegible]	[illegible]	[illegible]	[illegible]
[illegible]	[illegible]	[illegible]	[illegible]	[illegible]	[illegible]	[illegible]	[illegible]	[illegible]	[illegible]
[illegible]	[illegible]	[illegible]	[illegible]	[illegible]	[illegible]	[illegible]	[illegible]	[illegible]	[illegible]
Total.	[illegible]	[illegible]	[illegible]	[illegible]	[illegible]	[illegible]	[illegible]	[illegible]	[illegible]
[illegible]	[illegible]	[illegible]	[illegible]	[illegible]	[illegible]	[illegible]	[illegible]	[illegible]	[illegible]

[illegible]

[illegible]				
[illegible]	[illegible]	[illegible]	[illegible]	
[illegible]			[illegible]	
[illegible]	[illegible]		[illegible]	
[illegible]	[illegible]		[illegible]	
[illegible]	[illegible]	[illegible]	[illegible]	
Total.	[illegible]	[illegible]	[illegible]	
[illegible]				
[illegible]				
[illegible]		[illegible]	[illegible]	
[illegible]		[illegible]	[illegible]	
[illegible]	[illegible]	[illegible]	[illegible]	
Total.	[illegible]	[illegible]	[illegible]	
[illegible]				
[illegible]	[illegible]	[illegible]	[illegible]	
[illegible]	[illegible]	[illegible]	[illegible]	
[illegible]		[illegible]	[illegible]	
[illegible]	[illegible]		[illegible]	
[illegible]	[illegible]		[illegible]	
[illegible]				
[illegible]				
[illegible]				
[illegible]				
[illegible]	[illegible]	[illegible]	[illegible]	
[illegible]	[illegible]	[illegible]		

5.—Reformatory Schools.—Return showing the Number of Admissions, Discharges, and Modes of Discharge from 1859 to 1898.

—	Total. Boys.	Total. Girls.	Gross Total.
Admissions.			
1859, . .	96	44	140
1860, . .	178	68	246
1861, . .	137	59	196
1862, . .	141	30	171
1863, . .	119	62	181
1864, . .	119	46	165
1865, . .	118	42	160
1866, . .	136	27	163
1867, . .	164	40	204
1868, . .	218	48	266
1869, . .	215	44	259
1870, . .	220	45	265
1871, . .	235	51	286
1872, . .	249	58	307
1873, . .	250	44	294
1874, . .	219	65	284
1875, . .	198	46	244
1876, . .	188	57	245
1877, . .	210	65	275
1878, . .	228	40	268
1879, . .	221	44	265
1880, . .	243	53	296
1881, . .	231	38	269
1882, . .	278	41	319
1883, . .	196	54	250
1884, . .	199	45	244
1885, . .	148	16	164
1886, . .	175	30	205
1887, . .	146	32	178
1888, . .	183	40	223
1889, . .	245	28	273
1890, . .	127	19	146
1891, . .	141	21	162
1892, . .	131	14	145
1893, . .	110	28	138
1894, . .	120	15	135
1895, . .	112	10	122
1896, . .	110	9	119
1897, . .	157	16	173
1898, . .	180	16	196
Total, .	7,069	1,539	8,608

—	Total. Boys.	Total. Girls.	Gross Total.
Discharges.			
To employment or service,	2,034	500	2,534
To friends, . . .	2,449	584	3,033
Emigrated, . . .	967	161	1,128
Sent to sea, . . .	143	–	143
Enlisted, . . .	449	–	449
Discharged as diseased, .	53	26	79
Discharged as incorrigible or sentenced to penal servitude, . . .	51	10	61
Transferred, . . .	115	97	212
Died, ...	174	37	211
Absconded, sentence expired, ...	80	8	88
Total, . .	6,520	1,484	8,004
Under detention, 31st Dec., 1898, . . .	548	54	602
Viz.:			
In school, . . .	518	53	571
On licence, . . .	27	1	28
In prison, . . .	–	–	–
Absconded, sentence unexpired, . . .	3	–	3
Retained in school, sentence expired, . .	–	–	–

There was one boy admitted, in November, 1898, into Philipstown Reformatory School whose sentence was quashed in 1899, and who, therefore, should not have been included amongst the admissions in 1898.

Image digitised by the University of Southampton Library Digitisation Unit

7.—Reformatory Schools.—Returns of Receipts

Receipts and Expenditure.	Boys. Malone, Belfast.			Boys. Philipstown, King's Co.			Boys. St. Kevin's, Glencree, Co. Wicklow.		
Receipts.	£	s.	d.	£	s.	d.	£	s.	d.
Treasury Allowances,	1,180	2	0	4,178	8	3	2,828	17	9
Subscriptions, Legacies, Donations, &c.,	61	6	6	34	1	0	168	7	9
Payments from County and Borough Rates,	467	10	7	1,875	15	8	1,445	14	6
Sale of Labour,	—			—			—		
Sundries,	18	2	6	—			—		
Total Receipts,	1,789	15	6	6,878	18	9	4,465	19	2
Expenditure.									
Ordinary Charges.									
Officers' Pay (Salaries and House Wages),	363	16	6	896	8	0	793	13	0
Provisions (Officers),	118	0	8	445	8	6	400	8	0
" (Boys or Girls),	782	10	8	2,288	18	2	1,847	18	2
Clothing of Inmates,	188	1	10	783	15	6	381	14	8
Washing, Fuel, and Light,	279	10	2	857	9	6	580	13	9
Repairs, Rents and Taxes,	142	14	5	828	7	6	341	19	4
Furniture and House Sundries,	46	16	3	716	3	0	139	19	8
Printing and Office Expenses,	72	19	5	150	8	4	38	8	7
Travelling and Police Charges,	14	5	1	95	1	6	128	11	2
Medical Expenses, Funerals, &c.	48	14	4	114	12	0	62	13	8
Sundries, Rewards, &c.,	115	8	0	368	16	3	186	4	4
Total Ordinary Charges,	1,568	18	8	8,003	15	2	4,254	14	9
Extra Charges.									
Rent of School Premises,	63	5	5	55	0	0	—		
Interest,	—			120	0	0	—		
Disposal, Home,	76	18	10	150	5	0	131	2	8
" Emigration,	—			30	0	0	2	4	3
Building and Land,	—			98	4	0	143	2	4

...ts, and **Expenditure** for, the year 1888.

GIRLS. High Park, Dublin.	GIRLS. St. Joseph's, Limerick.	GIRLS. Spark's Lake, Monaghan.	Receipts and Expenditure.
£ s. d.	£ s. d.	£ s. d.	**Receipts.**
487 13 8	410 12 0	111 8 4	Treasury Allowances.
12 16 9	—	—	Subscriptions, Legacies, Donations, &c.
221 1 3	184 12 0	47 3 6	Payments from County and Borough Rates.
—	—	—	Hire of Labour.
—	24 10 0	—	Sundries.
702 12 8	569 14 0	158 13 0	Total Receipts.
			Expenditure.
			Ordinary Charges.
175 0 0	180 0 0	80 0 0	Officers' Pay (Salaries and House Wages).
—	—	—	Provisions (Officers).
341 0 0	277 7 8	104 12 6	(Boys or Girls).
34 2 0	57 0 11	3 12 9	Clothing of Inmates.
90 0 0	72 19 8	16 0 0	Washing, Fuel, and Light.
30 0 0	27 9 8	7 18 6	Repairs, Rates, and Taxes.
—	22 3 10	1 10 0	Furniture and House Sundries.
5 17 2	18 15 6	0 15 0	Printing and Office Expenses.
1 11 0	—	—	Travelling and Police Charges.
16 0 0	14 1 4	—	Medical Expenses, Funerals, &c.
—	36 15 9	4 0 0	Sundries, Rewards, &c.
365 10 2	728 14 8	198 11 3	Total Ordinary Charges.
			Extra Charges.
70 0 0	40 0 0	15 0 0	Rent of School Premises.
100 0 0	38 4 8	—	Interest.
48 15 0	34 14 2	6 10 0	Disposal, Home.
—	—	—	Emigration.
—	162 2 6	—	Building and Land.
218 15 0	275 1 0	21 10 0	Total Extra Charges.
714 5 2	997 15 8	220 1 3	Total Expenditure.
28 18 0	128 0 7	5 1 0	Profit (including Stock on Lands and Bills).
—	—	—	Loss.

[illegible]

[illegible]	[illegible]	[illegible]	[illegible]	[illegible]	[illegible]	[illegible]	[illegible]	[illegible]	[illegible]
	£ s. d.	£ s. d.	£ s. d.	£ s. d.	£ s. d.	£ s. d.	£ s. d.		£ s. d.
[illegible]	[illegible]	[illegible]	[illegible]	[illegible]	[illegible]	–	[illegible]	[illegible]	[illegible]
[illegible]	[illegible]	[illegible]	[illegible]	[illegible]	[illegible]	–	[illegible]	[illegible]	[illegible]
[illegible]	[illegible]	–	[illegible]	[illegible]	[illegible]	–	[illegible]	[illegible]	[illegible]
[illegible]	[illegible]	[illegible]	[illegible]	[illegible]	[illegible]	–	[illegible]	[illegible]	[illegible]
[illegible]	[illegible]	[illegible]	[illegible]	[illegible]	[illegible]	–	[illegible]	[illegible]	[illegible]
[illegible]	[illegible]	[illegible]	[illegible]	[illegible]	[illegible]	–	[illegible]	[illegible]	[illegible]
Total	[illegible]	[illegible]	[illegible]	[illegible]	[illegible]	–	[illegible]	–	

INDUSTRIAL SCHOOLS.

9.—INDUSTRIAL SCHOOLS:—RETURN of ADMISSIONS,

—	"[illegible]" Training Ship, Belfast.	Balmoral, Belfast.	Hampton House, Belfast.	St. Patrick's, [illegible], Belfast.	St. Patrick's, Crumlin-road, Belfast.	Abbeyville, White Abbey, Belfast.	Shamrock Lodge, Belfast.	Middletown, co. Armagh.	Lurgan.	St Joseph's, Cavan.	[illegible]	St. Aloysius, Clonakilty.	St. [illegible], [illegible]	Our Lady of Mercy, Kinsale.
	B.	B.	G.	B.	G.	G.	G.	B.	G.	G.	G.	G.	G.	G.
Under Detention, 31st Dec., 1897:—														
In School (within number paid for under rules).	226	100	138	160	110	60	96	60	30	87	73	130	48	120
" (In excess of number paid for, or under 6 years).	–	16	11	4	2	2	3	6	4	1	1	8	1	2
On Licence,	9	13	11	14	16	–	10	4	4	7	–	5	6	10
Absconded, Sentence unexpired,	–	1	–	–	–	–	–	–	–	–	–	–	–	–
Retained in School, Sentence expired,	–	1	1	–	–	–	3	–	–	1	–	3	–	–
Total,	235	131	161	198	128	62	109	69	38	96	75	144	55	132
Admitted by Committment in 1898,	34	32	47	37	27	10	14	12	6	5	23	21	6	18
" Transfer,	31	–	–	–	–	27	–	–	–	–	–	–	–	–
" Recommitted,	–	–	–	–	–	–	–	–	–	–	–	–	–	–
Total,	65	32	47	37	27	37	14	14	6	5	23	21	6	18
Discharged, Transferred, or Died in 1898,	62	31	38	30	31	2	14	8	14	15	19	19	6	17
Under Detention, 31st December, 1898:—														
In School (within number paid for under rules).	216	100	150	150	97	80	90	60	45	75	60	120	46	120
" (In excess of number paid for, under 6 years).	–	16	22	6	1	3	7	10	2	2	3	14	–	4
On Licence,	12	16	10	8	17	4	7	8	6	6	–	8	9	8
Absconded, Sentence unexpired,	1	–	–	–	–	–	–	–	–	–	–	–	–	–
Retained in School, Sentence expired,	–	–	–	–	5	1	1	1	–	1	–	2	–	–
Total,	238	132	182	164	120	88	105	66	37	86	83	146	56	133
AVERAGE NUMBER OF CHILDREN.														
(i.) Inmates under Orders of Detention and paid for by Treasury,	240·83	100	136	132	97·1	61·1	88	60	46	78	80	120	46	120
(ii.) Inmates under Orders of Detention but as yet not chargeable to the Treasury, being under 6 years of age.	–	3	14	–	1	2·1	3	6	1	2	2	5·2	–	7·6
(iii.) Inmates above the age of 6 years under Orders of Detention but as yet not chargeable to the Treasury, being in excess of the number fixed by the rules of the School.	–	6	2	27	–	–	5	10	–	–	–	2·8	–	–
(iv.) Voluntary Inmates (Inmates not under Orders of Detention) supported by the Managers out of funds other than those received from the Treasury.	–	–	2	6	7	14	13	1	–	6	–	–	3	–
Total,	240·83	112	170	165	98	96	104	84	46	86	82	133·2	49	140·5
Average Number of Externs attending the School.	–	–	–	–	–	–	–	100	–	–	100	–	100	–

[illegible]	[illegible]	[illegible]
[illegible]	[illegible]	[illegible]
[illegible]	[illegible]	[illegible]
[illegible]	[illegible]	[illegible]
[illegible]	[illegible]	[illegible]
[illegible]	[illegible]	[illegible]
[illegible]	[illegible]	[illegible]
[illegible]	[illegible]	[illegible]
[illegible]	[illegible]	[illegible]
[illegible]	[illegible]	[illegible]
[illegible]	[illegible]	[illegible]
[illegible]	[illegible]	[illegible]
[illegible]	[illegible]	[illegible]
[illegible]	[illegible]	[illegible]
[illegible]	[illegible]	[illegible]
[illegible]	[illegible]	[illegible]
[illegible]	[illegible]	[illegible]
[illegible]	[illegible]	[illegible]
[illegible]	[illegible]	[illegible]

9.—Industrial Schools.—Return of Admissions,

—	St. Anne's, Galway.	Salthill, Galway.	St. Joseph's Home, Kilkenny.		St. Joseph's, Tralee.	Pembroke Alms-house, Tralee.	Kilkenny Male.	Kilkenny Female.	St. John's, Parsonstown.	St. George's, Limerick.	St. Vincent's, Limerick.
	G.	B.	B.	G.	B.	G.	B.	G.	G.	G.	G.
Under Detention, 31st Dec., 1887:—											
In School (within number paid for under rules).	77	190	[illegible]	75	109	67	165	166	75	160	[illegible]
" (In excess of number paid for, or under 6 years).	1	4	6	6	1	3	4	7	1	16	1
On Licence,	1	15	9	8	11	5	37	6	6	8	11
Absconded, Sentence unexpired,	–	–	–	–	–	–	–	–	–	–	–
Retained in School, Sentence expired,	1	1	–	–	–	2	–	6	1	–	1
Total,	[illegible]	[illegible]	31	87	118	[illegible]	[illegible]	118	82	119	[illegible]
Admitted by Commitment in 1888,	11	20	6	9	18	12	17	12	14	18	7
" Transfer,	–	9	–	–	1	–	–	–	–	–	–
" Re-committal,	–	–	–	–	–	–	–	–	–	–	–
Total,	11	29	6	9	[illegible]	13	17	12	16	[illegible]	[illegible]
Discharged, Transferred, or Died in 1888,	8	48	16	11	[illegible]	17	42	16	16	18	[illegible]
Under Detention, 31st December, 1888:—											
In School (within number paid for under rules).	77	[illegible]	22	72	[illegible]	70	160	106	77	160	[illegible]
" (in excess of number paid for, under 6 years).	6	–	–	–	–	1	4	6	–	11	
On Licence,	3	16	7	1	16	4	44	1	3	3	1
Absconded, Sentence unexpired,	–	–	–	–	–	–	–	–	–	–	–
Retained in School, Sentence expired,	–	–	–	–	–	1	–	6	1	–	
Total,	[illegible]	[illegible]	22	73	118	72	210	118	[illegible]	116	[illegible]

[illegible], &c., during the Year ending 31st December, [illegible]—continued.

[illegible]

16.—Industrial Schools.—Summary of Admissions, Discharges, &c., for the year ending 31st December, 1898.

—	Total. Boys.	Total. Girls.	Gross Total.
Under Detention, 31st December, 1897—			
In School (within number paid for under Rules),	3,441	4,321	7,762
" (in excess of number paid for, or under 6 years of age),	43	226	269
On Licence,	304	284	588
Absconded, Sentence unexpired,	5	–	5
Retained in School, Sentence expired,	22	79	101
Total,	3,872	4,910	8,782
Admitted in 1898,	606	631	1,236
" by Transfer,	140	50	190
" by Re-committal,	–	–	–
Total,	747	680	1,426
Discharged, Transferred, or Died in 1898,	758	719	1,477
Under Detention, 31st December, 1898—			
In School (within number paid for under Rules),	3,458	4,307	7,765
" (in excess of number paid for, or under 6 years),	91	208	299
On Licence,	345	249	594
Absconded, Sentence unexpired,	3	–	3
Retained in School, Sentence expired,	8	60	68
Total,	3,902	4,824	8,726
State of Instruction on Admission—			
Neither Read nor Write,	344	348	692
Read, or Read and Write imperfectly,	344	303	647
Read and Write well,	57	52	109
Superior Instruction,	–	–	–
Total,	745	683	1,428
Age at Admission—			
Under 6 years,	20	83	103
From 6 to 8,	144	149	293
" 8 to 10,	198	159	357
" 10 to 12,	171	144	315
" 12 to 14,	192	77	269
Total,	725	633	1,358
Mode of Discharge—			
To employment or service,	366	378	744
Returned to Friends,	158	218	376
Emigrated,	8	84	92
Sent to Sea,	16	–	16
Enlisted,	3	–	3
Specially discharged,	16	6	22
Committed to Reformatory,	4	–	4
Transferred,	140	35	175
Died,	17	51	68
Absconders discharged by expiration of sentence,	6	–	6
Discharged on account of insufficient grounds for detention,	7	11	18
Total,	758	719	1,477

II.—INDUSTRIAL SCHOOLS.—RETURN of PARTICULARS of ADMISSIONS and DISCHARGES, during the Year 1898.

—	"Grampian" Training Ship, Belfast.	Balmoral, Belfast.	Hampton House, Belfast.	St. Patrick's, Milltown, Belfast.	St. Patrick's, Donegall Road, Belfast.	Abbeyville, White Abbey, Belfast.	Shamrock Lodge, Belfast.	Middletown, co. Armagh.	Lurgan.	St. Joseph's, Cavan.	Ennis.	St. Aloysius', Clonakilty.	St. Coleman's, Queenstown.	Our Lady of Mercy, Kinsale.	Upton, co. Cork.	Boys' Home, [illegible], Cork.	Mallow.	Passage West.	Baltimore, co. Cork.	St. Finbarr's, [illegible], Cork.	Greenmount, Cork.	[illegible] Home, [illegible], Cork.	Killybegs, co. Donegal.	Artane, co. Dublin.
	B.	B.	G.	B.	G.	G.	G.	B.	G.	G.	G.	B.	G.	G.	B.	B.	G.	B.	B.	G.	B.	G.	B.	B.
STATE OF INSTRUCTION ON ADMISSION—																								
Neither Read nor Write,	10	14	8	15	32	6	10	12	8	7	11	11	2	6	5	6	4	26	7	13	8	4	4	82
Read or Write imperfectly.	40	11	32	17	4	4	4	3	1	1	12	13	3	8	7	3	4	–	5	16	8	6	–	54
Read and Write well,	8	–	8	–	–	–	1	–	–	–	–	–	–	1	3	1	1	–	5	–	3	1	–	13
Superior Instruction,	–	–	–	–	–	–	–	–	–	–	–	–	–	–	–	–	–	–	–	–	–	–	–	–
Total,	84	25	47	32	37	10	14	15	6	8	23	24	5	15	18	8	9	26	17	31	14	8	4	146
AGE AT ADMISSION—																								
Under 6 years,	–	5	11	–	6	1	1	3	1	2	2	4	1	5	–	–	1	8	–	3	–	3	–	–
From 6 to 8,	3	10	13	2	[illegible]	[illegible]	[illegible]	[illegible]	[illegible]	[illegible]	4	6	–	1	–	2	[illegible]	10	1	8	–	[illegible]	[illegible]	8
" 8 to 10,	[illegible]	8	4	10	[illegible]	[illegible]	[illegible]	[illegible]	[illegible]	[illegible]	[illegible]	[illegible]	1	4	[illegible]	3	[illegible]	4	4	11	3	7	1	40
" 10 to 12,	26	1	13	15	[illegible]	[illegible]	[illegible]	1	3	1	[illegible]	[illegible]	2	4	[illegible]	1	[illegible]	–	[illegible]	6	6	2	1	67
" 12 to 14,	22	–	4	2	[illegible]	1	[illegible]	1	–	–	5	1	1	3	3	3	–	–	3	5	6	3	–	33
Total,	84	25	47	32	37	10	14	15	6	8	23	24	5	15	18	8	9	26	17	31	14	8	4	146
MODE OF DISCHARGE—																								
To Employment or Service.	20	3	24	26	14	–	8	2	14	10	8	11	3	10	18	7	4	–	9	11	27	8	–	100
Returned to Friends,	21	4	7	8	9	2	3	3	–	9	4	4	1	6	10	7	–	1	4	1	11	1	8	25
Emigrated,	–	–	–	–	–	–	–	1	–	–	–	1	–	–	–	–	4	–	1	2	–	–	–	8
Sent to Sea,	10	1	–	–	–	–	–	–	–	–	–	–	–	–	–	1	–	–	4	–	–	–	–	–
Enlisted,	3	–	–	–	–	–	–	–	–	–	–	–	–	–	–	–	–	–	–	–	–	–	–	–
Specially discharged,	4	2	–	1	–	–	1	–	–	–	–	1	–	–	1	–	–	–	–	1	2	–	–	2
Committed to Reformatory.	–	1	–	–	–	–	–	–	–	–	–	–	–	–	–	–	–	–	1	–	–	–	–	–
Transferred,	–	21	–	–	26	–	1	–	–	–	–	–	–	–	–	–	–	27	–	–	2	–	2	–
Died,	5	–	1	1	2	1	1	2	–	–	2	1	–	1	1	–	3	–	–	2	1	–	–	2
Absconders discharged by expiration of sentence.	–	1	–	–	–	–	–	–	–	–	–	–	–	–	–	1	–	–	–	–	–	–	–	1
Discharged on account of insufficient grounds for Detention.	–	–	–	–	–	–	–	–	–	–	3	–	–	–	–	–	3	–	–	–	–	–	–	1
Total,	88	33	33	36	51	3	15	6	14	10	13	13	4	17	17	16	14	28	30	17	46	4	3	134

11.—Industrial Schools.—Return of Particulars of Admissions

—	Booterstown, co. Dublin.	St. Mary's, [illegible], co. Dublin.	Golden Bridge, co. Dublin.	Carriglea Park, co. Dublin.	St. Mary's, Lakelands, Sandymount, co. Dublin.	[illegible], co. Dublin.	[illegible], co. Dublin.	[illegible], co. Dublin.	St. [illegible], [illegible].	[illegible].	Clifden, co. Galway.	Letterfrack.	Oughterard, co. Galway.	St. Anne's, Galway.	Salt Hill, Galway.	St. Joseph's Home, Kilkenny.		St. Joseph's, Tralee.	[illegible], Tralee.	[illegible].	[illegible].
	G.	G.	G.	B.	G.	B.	B.	G.	G.	G.	B.	B.	G.	G.	B.	B.	G.	B.	G.	B.	G.
State of Instruction on Admission—																					
Neither Read nor Write,	4	5	6	11	8	6	13	1	7	8	6	14	1	8	16	8	8	9	6	21	9
Read or Write imperfectly.	–	10	16	11	5	12	18	1	1	8	4	2	5	8	13	8	1	7	9	13	5
Read and Write well,	1	–	3	–	–	5	–	–	1	–	1	–	2	–	1	–	–	–	–	–	4
Superior Instruction,	–	–	–	–	–	–	–	–	–	–	–	–	–	–	–	–	–	–	–	–	–
Total,	2	15	19	22	8	23	22	2	9	8	11	16	6	11	30	6	9	16	15	47	12
Age at Admission—																					
Under 6 years,	–	[illegible]	–	–	1	–	[illegible]	[illegible]	[illegible]	[illegible]	[illegible]	–	–	–	–	–	–	–	–	[illegible]	[illegible]
From 6 to 8,	1	[illegible]	6	–	[illegible]	[illegible]	[illegible]	1	[illegible]	[illegible]	1	[illegible]	1	[illegible]	[illegible]	[illegible]	[illegible]	–	[illegible]	[illegible]	[illegible]
" 8 to 10,	–	[illegible]	10	10	–	8	6	–	[illegible]	[illegible]	[illegible]	[illegible]	[illegible]	[illegible]	17	4	1	8	[illegible]	11	4
" 10 to 12,	–	[illegible]	[illegible]	[illegible]	4	[illegible]	[illegible]	–	2	[illegible]	[illegible]	[illegible]	[illegible]	[illegible]	11	–	–	[illegible]	[illegible]	–	[illegible]
" 12 to 14,	1	–	[illegible]	[illegible]	1	[illegible]	[illegible]	–	1	[illegible]	[illegible]	[illegible]	[illegible]	1	[illegible]	–	[illegible]	[illegible]	[illegible]	–	[illegible]
Total,	2	15	21	22	8	23	23	2	9	8	11	16	6	11	30	6	9	16	15	47	12
Mode of Discharge—																					
To Employment or Service.	3	12	8	16	9	22	17	5	8	6	8	12	8	8	34	–	7	14	6	–	9
Returned to Friends,	4	7	13	8	–	3	8	–	4	[illegible]	[illegible]	[illegible]	[illegible]	[illegible]	[illegible]	[illegible]	[illegible]	[illegible]	[illegible]	7	6
Emigrated,	–	–	–	–	–	–	–	–	–	–	[illegible]	–	[illegible]	–	[illegible]	–	[illegible]	–	[illegible]	–	–
Sent to Sea,	–	–	–	–	–	–	–	–	–	–	–	–	–	–	–	–	–	–	–	–	–
Enlisted,	–	–	–	–	–	–	–	–	–	–	–	–	–	–	–	–	–	–	–	–	–
Specially discharged,	–	1	–	–	–	–	–	–	–	–	–	–	–	–	–	–	–	–	–	–	–
Committed to Reformatory.	–	–	–	–	–	–	–	–	–	–	–	2	–	–	–	–	–	–	–	–	–
Transferred,	–	–	1	–	–	–	–	–	2	–	–	–	–	–	–	–	–	1	[illegible]	[illegible]	–
Died,	2	–	2	–	1	1	–	–	–	–	1	1	1	1	–	–	1	–	1	2	1
Absconders discharged by expiration of sentence.	–	–	–	–	–	–	–	–	–	–	–	–	–	–	–	–	–	–	–	–	–
Discharged on account of insufficient grounds for detention.	–	–	–	–	–	2	–	–	–	–	–	–	–	–	1	–	1	–	–	–	–
Total,	9	21	26	18	9	26	25	5	11	14	8	22	8	8	45	10	17	20	17	43	16

[illegible] during the Year [illegible]—continued.

[illegible]

sed by the University of Southampton Library Digitisation Unit

13.—Industrial Schools.—Return showing the Number of Admissions, Discharges, and Modes of Discharges, from 1869 to 1898.

—	Total. Boys.	Total. Girls.	Grand Total.
Admissions.			
1869, . . .	65	184	249
1870, . . .	258	1,171	1,429
1871, . . .	499	634	1,133
1872, . . .	725	296	1,021
1873, . . .	487	657	1,144
1874, . . .	456	601	1,057
1875, . . .	490	518	1,008
1876, . . .	367	493	860
1877, . . .	349	596	945
1878, . . .	666	199	865
1879, . . .	583	577	1,160
1880, . . .	774	830	1,603
1881, . . .	531	726	1,257
1882, . . .	611	752	1,363
1883, . . .	438	708	1,146
1884, . . .	601	703	1,304
1885, . . .	963	755	1,718
1886, . . .	723	906	1,629
1887, . . .	862	685	1,547
1888, . . .	666	771	1,437
1889, . . .	935	711	1,646
1890, . . .	752	789	1,541
1891, . . .	651	723	1,374
1892, . . .	891	704	1,595
1893, . . .	750	709	1,459
1894, . . .	751	675	1,426
1895, . . .	752	815	1,567
1896, . . .	687	789	1,476
1897, . . .	778	772	1,550
1898, . . .	747	663	1,410
Total, .	18,719	20,913	39,632

—	Total. Boys.	Total. Girls.	Grand Total.
Discharges.			
To employment or service,	6,209	8,711	14,920
To friends, . . .	2,921	3,945	6,866
Emigrated, . . .	455	1,166	1,621
Sent to sea, . . .	426	-	426
Enlisted, . . .	167	-	167
Discharged as diseased, .	357	201	558
Committed to reformatories, . . .	145	60	205
Transferred, . . .	3,202	481	3,683
Died, ...	705	1,168	1,873
Absconded—sentence expired, . . .	90	10	100
Discharged — committal illegal, . . .	180	317	497
Total, . .	14,857	16,059	30,916
Under detention, 31st Dec., 1898, . .	3,862	4,854	8,716
Viz.—			
In school, . .	3,508	4,543	8,051
On licence, . .	345	249	594
Absconded — sentence unexpired, . .	5	-	5
Retained in school—sentence expired, .	6	60	66

13.—INDUSTRIAL SCHOOLS.—Discharges for the years 1895, 1896, 1897, showing the number Doing Well, Convicted of Crime, &c., from their Discharge to 31st December, 1898.

—	"Gibraltar" Ship.	Balmoral, Belfast.	Hampton House.	Milltown, Belfast.	[illegible], Belfast.	Abbeyville.	[illegible], Belfast.	[illegible].	Lurgan.	Cavan.	[illegible].	[illegible].	Queenstown.	[illegible].
MODE OF DISCHARGE—														
To Employment,	84	9	39	61	99	–	15	16	18	18	22	37	13	46
Returned to Friends,	85	3	17	22	56	–	4	10	13	21	17	19	7	10
Emigrated,	–	–	–	1	3	–	8	2	–	1	–	4	1	3
Sent to Sea,	33	–	–	–	–	–	–	–	–	–	–	–	–	–
Enlisted,	4	–	–	–	–	–	–	–	–	–	–	–	–	–
Specially Discharged,	6	3	8	–	–	–	–	–	–	–	–	1	1	1
Absconded and not Recovered,	–	1	–	–		–		–	–	–	–	–	–	–
Total,	161	15	56	84	[illegible]	–	26	29	29	35	40	52	26	64
SUBSEQUENT CHARACTER—														
Since Dead,	8	2	–	3	1	–	–	5	1	–	1	9	–	–
Doing well,	133	10	53	77	58	–	26	23	28	35	39	46	26	61
Doubtful,	5	–	4	3	–	–	–	–	–	–	–	–	–	–
Convicted of Crime,	1	–	–	1	–	–	–	–	–	–	–	–	–	–
Unknown,	36	3	–	–	–	–	1	1	–	–	–	6	–	3
Recommitted to an Industrial School,	–	–	–	–	–	–	–	–	–	–	–	–	–	–
Total,	161	15	56	84	59	–	26	29	28	35	40	52	26	64

—	[illegible], Upton, Cork.	[illegible].	Mallow.	[illegible] West.	Ballinasloe.	Sunday's Well, Cork.	[illegible], Cork.	Training Home, Cork.	Killybegs.	Artane.	[illegible].	[illegible].	Golden Bridge.	Carriglea.	[illegible].
MODE OF DISCHARGE—															
To Employment,	66	81	11	–	38	45	60	14	–	366	27	11	43	41	23
Returned to Friends,	55	11	7	2	22	9	45	7	–	78	16	8	86	21	17
Emigrated,	1	–	6	–	4	4	3	–	–	8	1	1	1	–	–
Sent to Sea,	–	6	–	–	8	–	–	–	–	–	–	–	–	–	–
Enlisted,	2	–	–	–	–	–	–	–	–	1	–	–	–	1	–
Specially Discharged,	2	–	–	1	8	–	1	–	–	14	1	1	–	1	1
Absconded and not Recovered,	1	1	–	–	–	–	–	–	–	–	–	–	–	1	–
Total,	125	49	22	3	76	58	112	21	–	462	47	18	82	65	41
SUBSEQUENT CHARACTER—															
Since Dead,	1	2	–	–	–	1	–	–	–	7	6	3	–	5	1
Doing well,	120	40	98	3	61	56	108	21	–	413	40	14	27	63	40
Doubtful,	3	5	–	–	8	1	2	–	–	7	–	–	4	–	–
Convicted of Crime,	–	–	–	–	–	–	6	–	–	–	–	–	–	–	–
Unknown,	2	–	–	–	8	–	5	–	–	85	1	1	31	1	–
Recommitted to an Industrial School,	–	–	–	–	–	–	–	–	–	–	–	–	–	–	–
Total,	125	49	98	3	76	58	116	21	–	492	47	16	62	65	41

13.—INDUSTRIAL SCHOOLS.—Discharges for the years 1895, 1896, 1897, showing
31st December,

—	"Meath," Blackrock.	[illegible]	[illegible]-street, Dublin.	Loughrea.	Ballinasloe.	Clifden.	Letterfrack.	Oughterard.	St. Anne's, Galway.	Salthill, Galway.	Killarney.	
MODE OF DISCHARGE—												
To Employment,	35	59	9	19	7	12	36	5	25	82	1	29
Returned to Friends,	18	11	6	17	17	11	42	7	18	16	1	[illegible]
Emigrated,	2	–	–	6	2	6	1	–	2	8	–	4
Sent to Sea,	–	–	–	–	–	–	–	–	–	–	–	–
Enlisted,	2	–	–	–	–	–	–	–	–	–	–	–
Specially Discharged,	–	1	1	–	–	1	2	–	1	1	–	–
Absconded and not Recovered,	–	–	–	–	–	–	–	–	–	–	–	–
Total,	57	71	16	42	26	30	81	16	45	107	2	46
SUBSEQUENT CHARACTER—												
Since Dead,	1	1	–	–	–	1	2	–	3	–	–	1
Doing well,	37	66	15	42	26	29	64	13	42	98	2	37
Doubtful,	2	4	1	–	–	–	3	–	–	4	–	–
Convicted of Crime,	–	–	–	–	–	–	–	–	–	1	–	–
Unknown,	17	–	–	–	–	–	12	–	–	5	–	8
Recommitted to an Industrial School.	–	–	–	–	–	–	–	–	–	–	–	–
Total,	57	71	16	42	26	30	81	13	45	107	2	46

—	Ballaghaderreen.	[illegible]	[illegible]	Summerhill, Athy.	[illegible] Abbey.	Sligo.	Clonmel.	Templemore.	Cashel.	Thurles.	Tipperary.	[illegible]	Cappoquin.
MODE OF DISCHARGE—													
To Employment,	11	20	11	30	22	21	35	12	30	14	16	21	7
Returned to Friends,	26	11	8	16	7	35	58	16	19	8	8	30	3
Emigrated,	1	–	2	2	–	2	1	–	–	–	1	1	–
Sent to Sea,	–	–	–	–	–	–	–	–	–	–	–	–	–
Enlisted,	–	–	–	–	–	–	–	–	–	–	–	–	–
Specially Discharged,	3	–	–	1	–	–	–	1	1	1	3	–	2
Absconded and not Recovered,	–	–	–	–	–	–	–	–	–	–	–	–	–
Total,	41	32	21	54	30	58	94	32	49	18	29	52	7
SUBSEQUENT CHARACTER—													
Since Dead,	–	2	–	–	3	–	1	–	–	–	–	3	–
Doing well,	40	30	21	52	27	57	86	30	47	17	29	49	5
Doubtful,	1	–	–	1	–	2	–	–	–	1	–	–	–
Convicted of Crime,	–	–	–	–	–	–	–	–	–	–	–	–	–
Unknown,	–	–	–	–	–	–	8	2	2	–	–	–	2
Recommitted to an Industrial School.	–	–	–	–	–	–	–	–	–	–	–	–	–
Total,	41	32	21	54	30	59	95	32	49	18	29	52	7

the number Doing **Well, Convicted of Crime, &c., from their Discharge to** 1897—*continued.*

—	St. Joseph's, Tralee.	Pembroke Alms..., Tralee.	Killarney, Boys.	Killarney, Girls.	Passmetown.	St. George's, Limerick.	St. Vincent's, Limerick.	Limerick Male.	Newtownforbes.	Drogheda.	Dundalk.	Westport.
MODE OF DISCHARGE.—												
To Employment.	33	12	–	27	20	22	50	43	43	5	15	21
Returned to Friends.	8	9	8	12	11	11	18	24	20	12	15	28
Emigrated.	3	3	3	3	–	4	–	6	3	–	1	2
Sent to Sea.	1	–	–	–	–	–	–	–	–	–	–	–
Enlisted.	4	–	–	–	–	–	–	1	–	–	–	–
Specially Discharged.	2	–	1	–	–	–	2	–	–	2	–	–
Absconded and not Recovered.	–	–	–	–	–	–	–	–	–	–	–	–
Total.	42	33	12	41	31	28	70	74	69	20	33	51
SUBSEQUENT CHARACTER.—												
Since Dead.	2	2	–	–	1	–	2	2	1	1	1	1
Doing well.	42	27	7	36	30	28	67	64	63	14	30	50
Doubtful.	2	3	–	2	–	–	–	–	2	–	–	–
Convicted of Crime.	–	–	–	–	–	–	–	–	–	–	–	–
Unknown.	–	3	5	3	–	–	1	6	3	5	2	–
Recommitted to an Industrial School.	–	–	–	–	–	–	–	2	–	–	–	–
Total.	46	33	12	41	31	28	70	74	69	20	33	51

—	Waterford.	Meath.	New Ross.	Wexford.	Bray.	Balbriggan.	Total. Boys.	Total. Girls.	Grand Total.
MODE OF DISCHARGE.—									
To Employment.	35	17	22	25	22	–	1,012	1,157	2,169
Returned to Friends.	11	6	8	11	9	6	490	695	1,181
Emigrated.	1	–	1	3	1	–	42	86	128
Sent to Sea.	–	–	–	–	–	–	41	–	41
Enlisted.	–	–	–	–	–	–	16	–	15
Specially Discharged.	–	–	–	–	–	4	46	24	70
Absconded and not Recovered.	–	–	–	–	–	–	4	–	4
Total.	47	23	31	40	25	10	1,656	1,964	3,620
SUBSEQUENT CHARACTER.—									
Since Dead.	–	–	–	1	1	3	30	43	73
Doing well.	47	23	31	39	22	7	1,447	1,814	3,261
Doubtful.	–	–	–	–	2	–	35	56	91
Convicted of Crime.	–	–	–	–	–	–	3	–	3
Unknown.	–	–	–	–	–	–	137	79	216
Recommitted to an Industrial School.	–	–	–	–	–	1	4	–	4
Total.	47	23	31	40	25	10	1,656	1,964	3,620

14.—INDUSTRIAL SCHOOLS.—RETURN of RECEIPTS in

RECEIPTS AND EXPENDITURE.	"Grampian" Training Ship, BELFAST. Boys.	Balmoral, BELFAST. Boys.	Hampton House, BELFAST. Girls.	St. Patrick's, Milltown, BELFAST. Boys.	St. Patrick's, Crumlin-road, BELFAST. Girls.
	1.	2.	3.	4.	5.
Average Number of Children paid for by Treasury.	240·69	100	157	150	95·1
Average Number of Children under 6 years of age and not yet paid for by Treasury.	–	5	14	–	·1
Average Number of Children in excess of limit, and not yet paid for by Treasury.	–	5	9	2·7	–
Average Number of Voluntary Inmates.	–	–	3	6	·2
RECEIPTS.	£ s. d.	£ s. d.	£ s. d.	£ s. d.	£ s. d.
Treasury Allowances,	3,094 7 6	1,383 0 6	1,932 12 0	1,063 11 8	1,411 15 6
Subscriptions, Legacies, Donations, &c.	803 7 0	16 18 6	18 4 0	–	–
Payments from County and Borough Rates.	1,428 0 10	718 1 8	925 16 0	966 13 2	726 1 6
Payments for Voluntary Inmates.	–	–	10 5 8	–	–
Hire of Labour,	22 1 0	5 12	–	–	–
Sundries,	63 15 0	–	18 4 11	61 18 0	–
Total Receipts,	4,831 13 4	2,088 18 8	2,878 16 7	3,002 3 5	2,153 3 8
EXPENDITURE.					
Ordinary Charges.					
Officers' Pay (Salaries & House Wages).	1,266 7 6	284 10 0	285 19 6	848 16 8	180 0 0
Officers' Rations,	110 0 0	90 0 0	310 0 0	142 10 0	140 0 0
Food for Inmates,	1,237 19 6	630 11 8	792 8 11	971 0 6	420 10 0
Clothing of Inmates,	766 15 0	339 17 6	438 18 11	528 13 1	285 10 6
Washing, Fuel, and Light,	185 19 4	146 6 6	426 10 1	184 17 4	208 10 6
Repairs, Rates, and Taxes,	61 9 3	277 14 8	172 13 9	586 19 10	34 4 6
Furniture and House Sundries,	77 6 5	162 1 6	168 10 6	272 8 10	10 5 6
Printing and Office Expenses,	301 18 8	60 8 8	63 12 11	28 17 0	7 5 6
Travelling and Police Charges,	9 18 6	85 15 11	5 16 0	8 1 8	9 0 8
Medical Expenses, Funerals, &c.,	152 17 5	88 14 8	49 16 3	61 8 6	26 0 0
Sundries, Rewards, &c.,	91 11 4	73 19 1	57 15 11	88 1 10	20 5 6
Total Ordinary Charges,	4,369 17 8	2,191 9 4	2,600 17 2	3,003 8 9	1,651 18 6
Extra Charges.					
Rent of School Premises,	–	–	67 18 0	60 0 6	60 0 0
Interest,	–	–	83 17 8	–	170 0 0
Disposal, Home,	126 0 5	15 15 6	68 8 8	123 18 1	100 10 6
Emigration,	–	–	–	–	–
Building and Land,	217 18 6	–	104 6 5	–	–
Total Extra Charges,	343 18 8	15 15 6	274 2 1	173 18 –	350 10 6
Total Expenditure,	4,718 16 1	2,207 4 10	2,874 19 8	3,179 4 8	1,681 8 6
INDUSTRIAL DEPARTMENT					
Profit (including Stock on hand and Bills).	263 18 2	116 1 11	326 14 8	63 3 8	0 5 8
Loss, do.,	–	–	–	–	–

and Expenditure for the Year 1898.

Abbeyville, Whiteabbey, Belfast. Girls.	Shamrock Lodge, Belfast. Girls.	Middletown, Armagh. Girls.	Lisburn. Girls.	St. Joseph's, Belfast. Girls.	Receipts and Expenditure.
6.	7.	8.	9.	10.	
1[illegible]3	38	60	45	76	Average Number of Child[ren] paid for by Treasury.
8·1	3	*1	1	*2	Average Number of Child[ren] under 6 years of age, and [not] yet paid for by Treasury.
–	8	*10	–	–	Average Number of Child[ren] in excess of limit, and not paid for by Treasury.
1·4	*11	*1	–	6	Average Number of Volunt[ary] Inmates.
£ s. d.	£ s. d.	£ s. d.	£ s. d.	£ s. d.	Receipts.
358 0 6	1,314 18 0	631 16 8	620 17 6	1,089 11 6	Treasury Allowances.
–	27 0 9	–	–	–	Subscriptions, Legacies, Do[nations], &c.
818 0 [illegible]	570 10 6	270 0 6	272 10 11	175 11 2	Payments from County [and] Borough Rates.
40 0 0	–	–		50 0 0	Payments for Voluntary

14.—INDUSTRIAL SCHOOLS.—RETURN of RECEIPTS in,

RECEIPTS AND EXPENDITURE.	Ennis. Girls.			St. Aloysius', Clonakilty. Girls.			[illegible] Girls.			Our Lady of Mercy, Kinsale. Girls.			[illegible], Upton, Co. Cork. Boys.		
	11.			12.			13.			14.			15.		
Average Number of Children paid for by Treasury.	30			135			46			126			260		
Average Number of Children under 6 years of age, and not yet paid for by Treasury.	1			5·4			–			*2·5			–		
Average Number of Children in excess of limit, and not yet paid for by Treasury.	–			3·8			–			–			5		
Average Number of Voluntary Inmates.	–			–			·2			–			–		
RECEIPTS.	£	s.	d.	£	s.	d.	£	s.	d.	£	s.	d.	£	s.	d.
Treasury Allowances,	1,025	3	8	1,684	18	4	608	12	8	1,758	1	6	2,601	2	3
Subscriptions, Legacies, Donations, &c.	–			–			20	4	0	–			–		
Payments from County and Borough Rates.	375	17	8	856	7	10	271	19	8	964	1	2	1,217	19	[illegible]
Payments for Voluntary In-	–			–			–			–			–		

and EXPENDITURE for the Year 1898—*continued.*

[illegible] Hill, Cork. Boys.	Malahide. Girls.	Passage West. Boys.	Baltimore, Co. Cork. Boys.	RECEIPTS AND EXPENDITURE.
16.	17.	18.	19.	
84	60	50	148	Average Number of Children paid for by Treasury.
–	*2	1	–	Average Number of Children under 6 years of age, and not yet paid for by Treasury.
–	*1	–	–	Average Number of Children in excess of Limit, and not yet paid for by Treasury.
–	*4	10	–	Average Number of Voluntary Inmates.
				RECEIPTS.
£ s. d.	£ s. d.	£ s. d.	£ s. d.	
712 9 3	780 3 5	644 7 1	1,848 0 3	Treasury Allowance.
254 18 9	–	40 0 0	13 9 0	Subscriptions, Legacies, Donations, &c.
229 5 6	490 1 6	306 18 1	884 9 1	Payments from County and Borough Rates.
–	–	130 0 0	–	Payments for Voluntary Inmates.
–	–	–	–	Hire of Labour.
–	–	–	5 10 0	Sundries.
1,196 13 6	1,281 4 11	1,128 5 2	2,746 4 4	Total Receipts.
				EXPENDITURE.
				Ordinary Charges.
241 19 3	66 0 0	48 0 0	478 15 7	Officers' Pay (Salaries & House Wages).
22 18 4	44 0 0	60 0 0	142 2 9	Officers' Rations.
402 5 2	560 16 7	484 0 0	988 4 9	Food for Inmates.
106 9 11	236 17 4	139 0 0	380 5 4	Clothing of Inmates.
85 10 9	116 17 8	106 0 0	178 17 1	Washing, Fuel, and Light.
6 13 3	60 3 7	50 0 0	38 8 6	Repairs, Rates, and Taxes.
7 17 8	31 0 11	35 0 0	32 5 3	Furniture and House Sundries.
5 9 0	11 15 9	23 10 8	18 13 9	Printing and Office Expenses.
3 19 9	3 18 3	3 10 0	–	Travelling and Police Charges.
5 7 2	26 19 5	25 0 0	44 6 8	Medical Expenses, Funerals, &c.
30 9 11	9 13 8	13 0 0	33 17 7	Sundries, Rewards, &c.
1,018 17 2	1,145 1 5	1,184 0 0	2,169 16 10	Total Ordinary Charges.
				Extra Charges.
166 0 0	–	35 0 0	31 10 0	Rent of School Premises.
44 10 3	110 0 0	25 0 0	20 0 8	Interest.
44 14 8	60 0 0	21 0 0	41 11 10	Disposal, Home.
–	24 0 0	–	–	„ Emigration.
–	–	28 0 0	36 7 7	Building and Land.
254 8 3	194 0 0	149 0 0	129 7 11	Total Extra Charges.
1,270 5 10	1,339 1 5	1,293 0 0	2,348 16 9	Total Expenditure.
				INDUSTRIAL DEPARTMENT.
248 17 0	61 18 8	14 0 0	144 0 11½	Profit (including Stock on hand and Bills).
–	–	–	–	Loss, do.

* Cost of maintenance not included in expenditure.

14.—Industrial Schools.—Return of Receipts in,

Receipts and Expenditure.	St. Finbar's, Cork. Girls. 20.	Greenmount, Cork. Boys. 31.	Training Home, Whitehall, Dublin. Girls. 32.	Killybegs, Donegal. Girls. 33.	Artane, Co. Dublin. Boys. 34.
Average Number of Children paid for by Treasury.	172	199	37	100	739
Average Number of Children under 6 years of age, and not yet paid for by Treasury.	10	·8	1·5	–	–
Average Number of Children in excess of limit, and not yet paid for by Treasury.	16	1·7	–	–	–
Average Number of Voluntary Inmates.	3	–	5	*1	1
Receipts.	£ s. d.	£ s. d.	£ s. d.	£ s. d.	£ s. d.
Treasury Allowances,	2,240 8 3	2,551 9 6	404 4 9	1,307 18 3	10,416 11 2
Subscriptions, Legacies, Donations, &c.	118 4 2	79 10 6	–	–	733 7 4
Payments from County and Borough Rates.	670 1 3	1,056 17 11	140 7 0	468 18 10	4,839 18 6
Payments for Voluntary Inmates.	45 0 0	–	70 0 0	9 7 8	19 13 9
Hire of Labour,	–	–	–	–	–
Sundries,	133 12 0	–	15 10 0	–	78 8 9
Total Receipts,	3,206 1 1	3,730 17 6	[illegible] 1 9	1,786 10 11	16,648 18 0
Expenditure.					
Ordinary Charges.					
Officers' Pay (Salaries & House Wages).	808 0 0	606 5 0	60 0 0	428 19 8	3,671 0 0
Officers' Rations,	246 0 0	250 0 6	72 0 0	100 5 [illegible]	645 0 0
Food for Inmates,	1,412 3 5	1,433 19 0	377 0 10	612 10 4	5,826 2 8
Clothing of Inmates,	372 14 9	474 4 7	73 4 0	288 7 8	2,315 11 9
Washing, Fuel, and Light,	223 13 10	221 3 8	120 16 11	104 19 9	865 18 1
Repairs, Rates, and Taxes,	106 9 4	176 10 0	63 1 4	22 12 6	836 9 1
Furniture and House Sundries,	404 15 11	91 10 9	7 10 6	59 17 3	952 17 8
Printing and Office Expenses,	34 0 10	61 10 0	9 5 8	8 18 3	323 19 0
Travelling and Police Charges,	14 19 9	6 15 8	–	–	161 4 4
Medical Expenses, Funerals, &c.,	64 9 4	63 17 4	3 13 9	90 16 4	342 17 8
Sundries, Rewards, &c.,	15 8 6	32 0 9	52 2 0	5 4 0	501 10 8
Total Ordinary Charges,	3,204 3 8	3,404 6 7	829 0 7	1,767 9 7	15,541 14 4
Extra Charges.					
Rent of School Premises,	91 10 0	25 10 0	70 0 0	3 15 0	150 0 0
Interest,	–	90 6 9	–	48 7 5	1,758 7 8
Disposal, Home,	87 14 0	105 5 9	8 16 0	1 18 6	[illegible] 3 8
" Emigration,	25 0 0	–	–	–	–
Building and Land,	–	170 19 6	–	–	184 13 11
Total Extra Charges,	204 4 9	391 7 0	78 16 0	54 1 0	2,857 6 7
Total Expenditure,	3,408 7 8	3,995 13 7	907 10 7	1,821 10 7	17,396 17 11
Industrial Department.					
Profit (including Stock on hand and Bills).	163 3 7	351 8 8	72 0 4	48 10 0	1,111 10 8
Loss, do.,	–	–	–	–	–

* Cost of maintenance not included in expenditure.

and EXPENDITURE for, the Year 1868—*continued*.

[illegible], Co. Donegal. Girls.	St. Mary's, [illegible], Co. [illegible]. Girls.	[illegible] Bridge, Co. Donegal. Girls.	[illegible] Park, Co. [illegible]. Boys.	RECEIPTS AND EXPENDITURE.
25.	26.	27.	28.	
64	79	140	151	Average Number of Children paid for by Treasury.
–	1	–	–	Average Number of Children under 6 years of Age, and not yet paid for by Treasury.
8	–	8	–	Average Number of Children in excess of limit, and not yet paid for by Treasury.
–	–	–	1	Average Number of Voluntary Inmates.
£ s. d.	£ s. d.	£ s. d.	£ s. d.	RECEIPTS.
703 10 0	1,042 16 3	1,853 7 6	1,904 16 0	Treasury Allowances.
–	60 0 0	–	119 17 0	Subscriptions, Legacies, Donations, &c.
330 1 7	416 0 10	905 4 7	608 15 2	Payments from County and Borough Rates.
–	–	–	13 6 8	Payments for Voluntary Inmates.
–	–	–	–	Hire of Labour.
92 4 0	–	–	14 18 0	Sundries.
1,126 4 7	1,518 17 1	2,758 12 1	2,808 12 10	Total Receipts.
				EXPENDITURE.
				Ordinary Charges.
29 0 0	99 0 0	107 8 8	1,012 11 4	Officers' Pay (Salaries & House Wages).
30 0 0	–	222 9 0	228 8 4	Officers' Rations.
587 3 1	800 3 6	1,117 18 3½	1,041 18 8	Food for Inmates.
57 5 2	178 4 8	267 15 11½	278 12 10	Clothing of Inmates.
150 15 1	140 12 0	107 17 8	210 3 10	Washing, Fuel, and Light.
66 19 0	106 6 4	202 16 8	73 2 5	Repairs, Rates, and Taxes.
20 0 0	38 4 0	84 15 7½	74 3 10	Furniture and House Sundries.
8 8 4	15 6 6	34 14 6½	68 7 5	Printing and Office Expenses.
2 0 0	12 9 0	19 2 7	41 8 8	Travelling and Police Charges.
16 1 2	24 5 8	66 18 4	72 15 7	Medical Expenses, Funerals, &c.
18 0 0	40 13 6	104 4 2½	82 11 5	Sundries, Rewards, &c.
1,040 11 10	1,342 15 6	2,455 13 8½	3,154 12 5	Total Ordinary Charges.
				Extra Charges.
87 17 6	80 0 0	183 17 5	167 6 8	Rent of School Premises.
–	–	356 3 4	401 0 0	Interest.
21 0 0	61 0 0	64 11 6	44 0 0	Disposal, Homes.
–	–	–	–	Emigration.
–	–	–	393 5 1	Building and Land.
88 17 6	141 0 0	604 12 3	1,056 5 9	Total Extra Charges.
1,129 9 4	1,483 15 6	3,060 4 4½	4,210 18 0	Total Expenditure.
				INDUSTRIAL DEPARTMENT.
9 4 11	178 12 4	162 18 11	–	Profit (including Stock on hand and Bills).
–	–	–	85 9 11	Loss, do.

14.—Industrial Schools.—Return of Receipts in,

Receipts and Expenditure.	St. Mary's, Lakelands, Sandymount, Co. Dublin. Girls.	Meath, Blackrock, Co. Dublin. Boys.	Merrion, Co. Dublin. Girls.	[illegible], Dublin. Girls.	St. Bridget's, Loughrea. Girls.
	59.	60.	61.	62.	63.
Average Number of Children paid for by Treasury.	70	123	149	79	118
Average Number of Children under 6 years of age, and not yet paid for by Treasury.	*1	–	1	3	1
Average Number of Children in excess of limit, and not yet paid for by Treasury.	–	–	3	–	–
Average Number of Voluntary Inmates.	–	–	·	1	*24
Receipts.	£ s. d.	£ s. d.	£ s. d.	£ s. d.	£ s. d.
Treasury Allowances,	907 6 3	1,607 0 5	1,853 8 9	417 17 6	1,651 10 6
Subscriptions, Legacies, Donations, &c.	–	201 5 0	12 16 0	33 16 7	
Payments from County and Borough Rates.	859 9 10	682 11 7	778 14 5	165 3 7	364 17 11
Payments for Voluntary Inmates.	–	–	–	–	–
Hire of Labour,	–	–	50 0 0	–	–
Sundries,	–	16 13 4	–	0 8 5	–
Total Receipts,	1,250 16 1	2,420 10 5	2,750 16 9	616 4 11	2,016 7 11
Expenditure.					
Ordinary Charges.					
Officers' Pay (Salaries & House Wages).	60 0 0	559 4 1	118 0 0	84 4 0	113 0 0
Officers' Rations,	66 0 0	10 0 0	850 0 0	65 0 0	110 0 0
Food for Inmates,	620 0 0	883 5 3	1,300 0 0	187 8 8	620 0 0
Clothing of Inmates,	138 0 0	322 19 3	380 0 0	70 8 9	290 0 0
Washing, Fuel, and Light,	125 0 0	161 16 7	300 0 0	79 9 5	110 0 0
Repairs, Rates, and Taxes,	45 0 0	87 17 11	310 0 0	25 16 8	60 0 0
Furniture and House Sundries,	55 0 0	140 6 1	50 0 0	4 18 0	100 0 0
Printing and Office Expenses,	12 0 0	50 8 5	15 0 0	5 5 10	12 0 0
Travelling and Police Charges,	3 10 0	7 6 0	–	1 1 8	15 0 0
Medical Expenses, Funerals, &c.,	28 0 0	44 5 9	146 0 0	19 8 0	10 0 0
Sundries, Rewards, &c.,	19 0 0	227 11 6	20 0 0	19 8 4	5 0 0
Total Ordinary Charges,	1,148 10 0	2,343 0 4	2,894 0 0	614 18 10	1,784 0 0
Extra Charges.					
Rent of School Premises,	92 0 0	32 5 8	50 0 0	39 0 0	80 0 0
Interest,	210 0 0	–	148 10 0	–	20 0 3
Disposal, Home,	28 0 0	52 4 1	60 0 0	11 6 1	30 0 0
" Emigration,	–	–	–	–	–
Building and Land,	–	–	–	–	40 0 0
Total Extra Charges,	330 0 0	84 9 9	252 10 0	43 6 1	170 0 0
Total Expenditure,	1,478 10 0	2,337 10 1	3,146 10 0	558 4 11	1,954 0 0
Industrial Department.					
Profit (including Stock on hand and Bills).	66 15 0	9 4 10	277 6 3	87 18 9	–
Loss, do.,	–	–	–	–	30 15 0

* Cost of maintenance not included in expenditure.

and EXPENDITURE for, the Year 1896—*continued*.

BALLINASLOE. Girls. 84.	CLIFDEN, Co. GALWAY. Girls. 85.	LETTERFRACK, GALWAY. Boys. 86.	OUGHTERARD, Co. GALWAY. Girls. 87.	RECEIPTS AND EXPENDITURE.
60	60	150	40	Average Number of Children paid for by Treasury.
-	6·1	-	-	Average Number of Children under 6 years of age, and not yet paid for by Treasury.
-	14·5	3	-	Average Number of Children in excess of limit, and not yet paid for by Treasury.
*3	-	-	-	Average number of Voluntary Inmates.
£ s. d.	£ s. d.	£ s. d.	£ s. d.	RECEIPTS.
763 6 8	1,043 17 6	1,949 6 9	616 14 9	Treasury Allowances.
-	130 0 10	-	-	Subscriptions, Legacies, Donations, &c.
551 7 8	480 2 10	773 16 11	207 4 6	Payments from County and Borough Cess.
-	-	-	-	Payments for Voluntary Inmates.
-	-	-	-	Hire of Labour.
-	-	-	-	Sundries.
1,316 10 11	1,653 1 2	2,723 3 8	723 10 6	Total Receipts.
				EXPENDITURE.
				Ordinary Charges.
50 0 0	190 17 0	479 10 0	110 0 0	Officers' Pay (Salaries & House Wages).
60 0 0	43 0 0	334 16 9	95 0 0	Officers' Rations.
620 0 0	832 4 2	1,194 14 11	242 10 6	Food for Inmates.
254 0 0	204 0 0	436 15 11	61 4 6	Clothing of Inmates.
108 10 0	160 0 0	116 10 1	95 6 6	Washing, Fuel, and Light.
30 0 0	60 0 0	197 2 5	30 14 7	Repairs, Rates, and Taxes.
65 13 0	41 13 0	262 19 8	19 8 1	Furniture and House Sundries.
5 0 0	23 0 0	23 12 3	5 16 6	Printing and Office Expenses.
9 0 0	-	57 14 11	1 1 6	Travelling and Police Charges.
40 0 0	11 0 0	41 1 7	19 9 5	Medical Expenses, Funerals, &c.
28 0 0	10 1 0	91 1 0	7 15 3	Sundries, Rewards, &c.
1,259 3 0	1,617 0 3	3,229 19 4	713 1 0	Total Ordinary Charges.
				Extra Charges.
96 0 0	60 0 0	-	60 0 0	Rent of School Premises.
25 0 0	18 0 0	260 0 0	-	Interest.
-	54 0 0	-	10 17 3	Disposal, Home.
60 0 0	5 13 0	-	5 0 0	" Emigration.
50 0 0	-	-	-	Building and Land.
231 0 0	137 13 0	260 0 0	75 17 5	Total Extra Charges.
1,470 3 0	1,764 15 3	3,482 19 4	788 18 5	Total Expenditure.
				INDUSTRIAL DEPARTMENT.
119 11 1	221 2 0	91 1 9	85 19 6	Profit (including Stock on hand and Bills).
-	-	-	-	Loss, do.

* Cost of maintenance not included in expenditure.

14.—INDUSTRIAL SCHOOLS.—RETURN of RECEIPTS in,

RECEIPTS AND EXPENDITURE.	St. Anne's, Galway, Girls.	Salthill, Galway, Boys.	St. Joseph's Home, Killarney, Boys.	St. Joseph's Home, Killarney, Girls.	St. Joseph's, Tralee, Boys.
	38.	39.	40.		41.
Average Number of Children paid for by Treasury.	77	205	25	78	100
Average Number of Children under 6 years of age, and not yet paid for by Treasury.	–	–	–	–	–
Average Number of Children in excess of limit, and not yet paid for by Treasury.	3	–	–	–	–
Average Number of Voluntary Inmates.	–	–	–	–	–
RECEIPTS.	£ s. d.	£ s. d.	£ s. d.	£ s. d.	£ s. d.
Treasury Allowances,	1,048 16 0	2,588 0 0	325 6 0	1,020 1 3	1,295 18 [illegible]
Subscriptions, Legacies, Donations, &c.	–	200 0 0	–	–	–
Payments from County and Borough Rates.	191 1 1	1,061 18 1	141 12 9	216 19 8	520 18 [illegible]
Payments for Voluntary Inmates.	–	–	–	–	–
Hire of Labour,	–		–	–	–
Sundries,	–	–	–	–	–
Total Receipts,	1,234 18 1	3,850 18 1	466 19 9	1,237 0 11	1,816 18 0
EXPENDITURE.					
Ordinary Charges.					
Officers' Pay (Salaries & House Wages).	140 0 0	548 15 0	40 0 0	100 0 0	383 4 0
Officers' Rations,	45 0 0	420 0 0	48 0 0	40 0 0	255 10 6
Food for Inmates,	620 0 0	1,800 3 8	110 3 8	380 14 4	806 8 7
Clothing of Inmates,	218 16 6	545 10 10	46 19 6	158 12 4	342 4 8
Washing, Fuel, and Light,	130 0 0	494 16 4	46 19 6	78 15 8	224 7 [illegible]
Repairs, Rates, and Taxes,	108 0 10	254 19 8	20 9 0	55 10 10	148 1 [illegible]
Furniture and House Sundries,	18 11 0	221 9 10	21 8 4	47 18 0	190 18 4
Printing and Office Expenses,	0 0 9	100 15 4	1 17 0	6 0 0	85 10 6
Travelling and Police Charges,	3 1 0	27 14 4	8 7 6	2 10 0	15 3 4
Medical Expenses, Funerals, &c.	18 0 0	58 3 1	1 10 0	6 10 0	50 15 6
Rewards, Bounties, &c.,	5 16 1	–	12 10 0	20 0 0	14 16 6
Total Ordinary Charges,	1,363 6 1	3,963 0 8	427 4 6	1,078 5 9	2,273 16 7
Extra Charges.					
Rent of School Premises,	126 0 0	158 17 0	2 0 0	7 0 0	–
Interest,	44 0 0	69 0 0	38 0 0	212 0 9	–
Disposal, House,	21 0 0	50 0 0	7 10 0	27 0 0	40 18 11
" Emigration,	–		–	8 10 0	–
Building and Land,	–	–	–	–	–
Total Extra Charges,	191 0 0	297 17 0	47 10 0	254 10 9	40 18 11
Total Expenditure,	1,554 6 1	4,261 0 8	474 14 6	1,333 16 6	2,314 15 6
INDUSTRIAL DEPARTMENT.					
Profit (including Stock on hand and Bills),	148 10 0	174 10 5	–	63 14 0	188 6 8
Loss, do.,	–	–	–	–	–

and EXPENDITURE for, the Year 1898—*continued.*

Pembroke Alms House, Tralee, Girls.	Kilkenny, Boys.	Killarney, Girls.	St. John's, Parsonstown, Girls.	Receipts and Expenditure.
42.	43.	44.	45.	
70	163	100	78·1	Average Number of Children paid for by Treasury.
*2	8	8	–	Average Number of Children under 6 years of age, and not yet paid for by Treasury.
–	1	4	–	Average Number of Children in excess of limit, and not yet paid for by Treasury.
–	8	–	*2	Average Number of Voluntary Inmates.
£ s. d.	£ s. d.	£ s. d.	£ s. d.	RECEIPTS.
876 0 0	2,187 10 11	1,308 11 9	1,004 16 5	Treasury Allowances.
–	95 10 0	–	–	Subscriptions, Legacies, Donations, &c.
169 5 1	670 16 11	488 14 6	307 11 3	Payments from County and Borough Rates.
–	–	–	–	Payments for Voluntary Inmates.
–	–	–	–	Hire of Labour.
–	–	–	–	Sundries.
1,045 5 1	3,101 17 10	1,797 6 5	1,313 6 8	Total Receipts.
				EXPENDITURE.
				Ordinary Charges.
60 0 0	303 8 0	141 0 0	185 3 10	Officers' Pay (Salaries & House Wages).
79 0 0	522 11 1	140 0 0	80 0 0	Officers' Rations.
438 0 0	1,331 16 9	1,051 9 8	628 7 1	Food for Inmates.
204 19 5	361 19 8½	211 16 6½	173 8 6	Clothing of Inmates.
59 2 0	203 11 6	276 1 10	120 8 9	Washing, Fuel, and Light.
73 9 0	11 1 6	190 6 4	72 4 4	Repairs, Rents, and Taxes.
46 8 2	126 9 8½	66 3 6	67 5 6	Furniture and House Sundries.
10 6 7	42 0 7	33 0 6½	21 16 10½	Printing and Office Expenses.
–	60 9 8½	7 0 0	1 4 8	Travelling and Police Charges.
63 10 2	37 16 6	94 3 6	9 6 4	Medical Expenses, Funerals, &c.
17 9 7	25 9 4	25 14 2	44 11 7	Sundries, Rewards, &c.
1,058 13 6	2,810 1 1½	2,225 14 11	1,335 7 5½	Total Ordinary Charges.
				Extra Charges.
–	78 5 6	17 0 0	78 11 10	Rent of School Premises.
–	209 1 8	234 10 0	–	Interest.
27 0 0	–	68 0 0	33 18 3	Disposal, Home.
17 0 0	–	–	–	" Emigration.
–	497 1 10½	120 14 6	–	Building and Land.
44 0 0	872 8 7½	406 4 8	112 5 1	Total Extra Charges.
1,086 13 6	3,782 9 9	2,631 19 5	1,447 12 6½	Total Expenditure.
				INDUSTRIAL DEPARTMENT.
50 0 4	180 13 9	863 6 8	118 8 6	Profit (including Stock on hand and Bills).
–	–	–	–	Loss, do.

* Cost of maintenance not included in expenditure.

14.—Industrial Schools.—Return of Receipts in,

Receipts and Expenditure.	St. George's, Limerick. Girls. 16.	St. Vincent's, Limerick. Girls. 17.	Limerick. Boys. 45.	Our Lady of Succour, Newtownforbes. Girls. 48.	House of Charity, Drumcondra. Boys. 50.
Average Number of Children paid for by Treasury.	100	160	169	144	91
Average Number of Children under 6 years of age, and not yet paid for by Treasury.	5	*5	–	*1	2
Average Number of Children in excess of limit, and not yet paid for by Treasury.	8	*8	–	–	1
Average Number of Voluntary Inmates.	–	*50	*1·75	–	3
Receipts.	£ s. d.	£ s. d.	£ s. d.	£ s. d.	£ s. d.
Treasury Allowances,	1,808 11 6	1,634 18 3	2,186 14 9	1,883 6 6	1,207 3 [illegible]
Subscriptions, Legacies, Donations, &c.	–	–	53 10 0	–	–
Payments from County and Borough Rates.	596 11 6	471 1 1	806 7 2	789 18 6	578 10 [illegible]
Payments for Voluntary Inmates.	6 15 6	–	10 0 0	–	40 0 0
Hire of Labour,	–	–	–	–	–
Sundries,	–	3 19 0	70 0 0	–	–
Total Receipts,	1,909 18 [illegible]	2,108 18 4	3,136 11 11	2,678 8 0	1,828 12 7
Expenditure.					
Ordinary Charges.					
Officers' Pay (Salaries & House Wages).	200 0 0	188 0 0	465 4 9	430 0 0	188 0 0
Officers' Rations,	–	187 0 0	293 0 0	–	197 0 0
Food for Inmates,	749 16 6	1,084 11 4	1,201 9 2	1,051 3 8	840 10 [illegible]
Clothing of Inmates,	20[illegible] 18 6	323 7 8	561 6 9	859 9 10	238 6 [illegible]
Washing, Fuel, and Light,	152 11 8	812 16 7	256 19 6	552 13 0	101 17 [illegible]
Repairs, Rates, and Taxes,	158 2 6	441 13 1	801 4 0	785 16 0	148 0 0
Furniture and House Sundries,	119 11 1[illegible]	109 18 [illegible]	78 4 9	181 10 11	88 10 0
Printing and Office Expenses,	32 8 6	20 0 0	11 10 4	64 9 1	18 10 0
Travelling and Police Charges,	–	3 18 6	12 10 [illegible]	–	8 4 [illegible]
Medical Expenses, Funerals, &c.,	47 4 4	69 16 10	47 0 11	61 14 4	85 0 0
Sundries, Rewards, &c.,	80 0 6	67 18 [illegible]	73 14 11	63 12 0	11 3 [illegible]
Total Ordinary Charges,	1,659 9 10	2,849 6 8	3,185 17 6	3,709 7 6	1,808 3 [illegible]
Extra Charges.					
Rent of School Premises,	90 9 [illegible]	60 0 0	58 3 5	35 0 0	14 0 [illegible]
Interest,	287 6 6	–	312 5 0	–	60 0 0
Disposal, Home,	56 18 2	114 0 0	58 19 8	101 18 8	–
" Emigration,	–	–	–	–	–
Building and Land,	168 7 6	–	75 0 0	–	–
Total Extra Charges	581 6 6	174 0 0	499 7 2	166 18 8	64 0 [illegible]
Total Expenditure,	2,240 15 6	3,023 6 8	3,685 4 8	3,409 0 8	1,872 3 6
Industrial Department.					
Profit (including Stock on hand and Bills).	93 11 1	162 5 10½	277 19 6	618 0 11½	16 6 6
Loss, do.,	–	–	–	–	–

* Cost of maintenance not included in expenditure.

and Expenditure for, the Year 1898—*continued.*

Dundalk. Girls.	St. Columba's, Westport. Girls.	Ballaghaderreen. Girls.	St. Martha's, Monaghan. Girls.	Receipts and Expenditure.
51.	52.	53.	54.	
80	108	73	67	Average Number of Childr paid for by Treasury.
*7	*1	8	3	Average Number of Childr under 6 years of age, and r yet paid for by Treasury.
*4	-	-	5	Average Number of Childr in excess of limit, and not y paid for by Treasury.
*15	*1	*2	-	Average Number of Volunta [i]nmates.
				Receipts.
£ s. d.	£ s. d.	£ s. d.	£ s. d.	
1,048 17 6	1,336 4 0	973 19 0	579 6 3	Treasury Allowances.
-	-	150 0 0	-	Subscriptions, Legacies, Don tions, &c.
598 11 6	541 1 11	548 4 10	304 14 3	Payments from County a Borough Rates.
-	-	-	-	Payments for Voluntary I

14.—Industrial Schools.—Return of Receipts in,

Receipts and Expenditure.	[illegible] Girls.	[illegible] Girls.	[illegible] Girls.	[illegible] Girls.
	55.	56.	57.	58.
Average Number of Children paid for by Treasury.	44	139	60	319
Average Number of Children under 6 years of age, and not yet paid for by Treasury.	-	8	*1	8
Average number of Children in excess of limit, and not yet paid for by Treasury.	8	1	-	-
Average Number of Voluntary Inmates.	24	40	-	47
Receipts.	£ s. d.	£ s. d.	£ s. d.	£ s. d.
Treasury Allowances,	516 11 9	1,780 14 8	651 16 0	1,839 1 8
Subscriptions, Legacies, Donations, &c.	-	8 15 0	-	-
Payments from County and Borough Rates.	236 8 5	743 4 9	259 3 9	659 3 3
Payments for Voluntary Inmates.	382 17 8	862 12 7	-	583 17 0
Hire of Labour,	-	-	-	-
Sundries,	-	44 10 6	-	-
Total Receipts,	1,161 15 10	2,897 18 9	910 19 9	3,088 1 5
Expenditure.				
Ordinary Charges.				
Officers' Pay (Salaries & House Wages).	105 0 0	583 8 7	96 0 0	279 0 0
Officers' Rations,	80 0 0	129 17 9	60 0 0	80 0 0
Food for Inmates,	612 14 4	1,218 18 1	405 10 0	1,461 14 0
Clothing of Inmates,	135 1 11	486 5 11	128 5 0	594 7 7
Washing, Fuel, and Light,	164 19 3	475 7 1	84 10 6	256 8 8
Repairs, Rent, and Taxes,	101 5 10	174 6 11	69 0 0	170 5 6
Furniture and House Sundries,	80 0 0	93 18 11	78 10 0	173 10 0
Printing and Office Expenses,	5 1 4	35 19 0	49 0 0	85 0 3
Travelling and Police Charges,	1 2 0	35 9 0	8 10 0	9 17 0
Medical Expenses, Funerals, &c.,	50 10 10	50 10 2	60 0 0	23 15 0
Sundries, Rewards, &c.,	22 0 0	19 18 6	10 0 0	74 10 0
Total Ordinary Charges,	1,277 12 11	3,033 14 11	1,018 5 6	3,040 7 6
Extra Charges.				
Rent of School Premises,	50 0 0	150 0 0	-	190 0 0
Interest,	-	17 10 0	75 10 0	85 15 2
Disposal, Home,	-	-	-	13 15 0
" Emigration,	-	-	-	-
Building and Land,	-	200 0 0	-	-
Total Extra Charges,	50 0 0	367 10 0	75 10 0	298 10 2
Total Expenditure,	1,327 12 11	3,401 4 11	1,093 15 6	3,338 17 8
Industrial Department.				
Profit (including Stock on hand and Bills).	-	319 14 8	118 19 6	265 11 1
Loss, do.,	67 0 6	-	-	-

* [illegible]

and Expenditure for, the Year 1898—*continued.*

[illegible] Boys.	St. Augustine's, [illegible] Girls.	St. [illegible], [illegible] Girls.	St. [illegible], [illegible] Girls.	Receipts and Expenditure.
59.	60.	61.	62.	
169·7	60	108·4	46	Average Number of Children paid for by Treasury.
-	1	-	-	Average Number of Children under 6 years of age, and not yet paid for by Treasury.
-	*6	-	-	Average Number of Children in excess of limit, and not yet paid for by Treasury.
1	*1	-	-	Average Number of Voluntary Inmates.
£ s. d.	£ s. d.	£ s. d.	£ s. d.	**Receipts.**
1,947 11 0	782 3 8	1,409 11 0	589 12 6	Treasury Allowances.
4 1 2	-	-	-	Subscriptions, Legacies, Donations, &c.
760 18 11	334 2 8	461 10 6	231 4 1	Payments from County and Borough Rates.
18 10 0	10 0 0	-	-	Payments from Voluntary Inmates.
18 18 6	-	-	-	Hire of Labour.
-	-	-	-	Sundries.
2,738 0 7	1,126 5 11	1,871 1 6	820 16 7	Total Receipts.
				Expenditure.
				Ordinary Charges.
446 14 6	83 0 0	22 0 0	110 0 0	Officers' Pay (Salaries & House Wages).
243 19 6	60 0 0	96 0 0	80 0 0	Officers' Rations.
975 8 8	438 11 9	741 17 4	290 10 0	Food for Inmates.
420 5 9	142 7 8	298 7 8	180 10 0	Clothing of Inmates.
191 3 4	166 18 6	257 15 9	69 13 0	Washing, Fuel, and Light.
46 16 8	156 1 10	299 18 0	22 17 6	Repairs, Rates, and Taxes.
160 18 9½	11 15 9½	54 15 7	40 2 6	Furniture and House Sundries.
70 17 9	10 1 5	69 13 6	10 0 0	Printing and Office Expenses.
-	3 2 8	6 18 7	-	Travelling and Police Charges.
27 4 6	15 3 11	37 4 2	10 0 0	Medical Expenses, Funerals, &c.
22 10 6	20 7 0½	29 7 4	15 0 0	Sundries, Rewards, &c.
2,610 3 4½	1,061 13 7	1,904 9 9	819 15 0	Total Ordinary Charges.
				Extra Charges.
-	60 0 0	51 18 3	-	Rent of School Premises.
158 18 4	90 0 0	35 0 0	18 0 0	Interest.
32 3 7	-	40 2 9	21 10 0	Disposal, Home.
3 7 6	-	-	-	" Emigration.
-	-	-	-	Building and Land.
194 9 5	150 0 0	126 15 11	39 10 0	Total Extra Charges.
2,804 10 9½	1,211 13 7	2,031 5 8	859 5 0	Total Expenditure.
				Industrial Department.
226 18 3	186 12 5	157 8 1	33 16 11	Profit (including Stock on hand and Bills).
-	-	-	-	Loss, do.

* Cost of maintenance not included in expenditure.

14.—Industrial Schools.—Return of Receipts in

Receipts and Expenditure.	Tipperary. Girls. 52.	St. Catherine's, Strabane. Girls. 61.	Cappoquin, Waterford. Boys. 62.	St. Dominick's, Waterford. Girls. 66.	Mount Carmel, Moate. Girls. 67.
Average Number of Children paid for by Treasury.	64	93	51	160	50·2
Average Number of Children under 6 years of age, and not yet paid for by Treasury.	*3·2	3	1	1	–
Average Number of Children in excess of limit, and not yet paid for by Treasury.	*3·7	–	1	–	–
Average Number of Voluntary Inmates.	*12·6	*2	1	4	–
Receipts.	£ s. d.	£ s. d.	£ s. d.	£ s. d.	£ s. d.
Treasury Allowances,	824 8 0	1,264 6 0	660 7 6	2,064 18 6	636 3 8
Subscriptions, Legacies, Donations, &c.	–	–	–	50 4 9	–
Payments from County and Borough Rates.	106 12 1	500 13 1	260 5 8	704 10 8	265 8 6
Payments for Voluntary Inmates.	48 8 0	–	25 12 0	–	–
Hire of Labour,	–	–	–	–	–
Sundries,	–	–	–	–	2 4 0
Total Receipts,	984 0 1	1,704 19 1	960 4 11	2,839 18 3	909 16 0
Expenditure.					
Ordinary Charges.					
Officers' Pay (Salaries & House Wages).	91 2 0	82 0 0	108 12 0	316 6 0	117 0 0
Officers' Rations,	118 11 0	–	84 0 0	158 0 0	80 0 0
Food for Inmates,	342 4 8	844 4 0	444 17 11	1,807 10 0	349 12 8
Clothing of Inmates,	149 15 2	186 15 2	109 0 8	402 6 2	149 4 6
Washing, Fuel, and Light,	109 8 8	113 0 0	121 11 8	215 8 1	99 14 0
Repairs, Rates, and Taxes,	15 1 10	208 16 4	27 6 6	600 12 4	22 10 7
Furniture and House Sundries,	42 0 8	117 14 8	32 12 6	164 4 10	21 10 5
Printing and Office Expenses,	5 9 0	17 10 8	13 6 1	35 8 11	5 2 2
Travelling and Police Charges,	–	1 18 8	2 12 4	8 7 0	–
Medical Expenses, Funerals, &c.	30 0 8	58 10 8	15 4 8	33 0 0	23 11 8
Sundries, Rewards, &c.,	11 4 0	17 6 2	20 10 4	30 10 7	11 17 0
Total Ordinary Charges,	1,092 11 11	1,637 14 6	976 17 1	3,052 18 11	840 2 7
Extra Charges.					
Rent of School Premises,	35 2 0	–	20 0 0	100 0 0	21 0 8
Interest,	215 12 0	142 10 0	–	150 0 0	100 0 8
Disposal: Home,	26 10 11	52 0 6	1 10 0	98 0 0	19 16 2
Emigration,	–	–	–	–	–
Building and Land,	–	–	–	–	46 11 10
Total Extra Charges,	277 3 5	194 10 6	21 10 0	398 0 0	186 8 5
Total Expenditure,	1,369 17 4	1,832 4 4	998 7 1	5,030 18 11	1,026 10 7
Industrial Department.					
Profit (including Stock on hand and Bills).	407 14 8	63 11 8	–	238 11 8	119 12 1
Loss, do.,	–	–	19 18 7	–	–

* Cost of maintenance not included in expenditure.

[Receipts] and Expenditure for, the Year 1898—*continued.*

St. Aidan's, New Ross. Girls.	St. Michael's, Wexford. Girls.	[illegible], Bray. Girls.	St. Kyran's, Rathdrum, Co. Wicklow. Boys.	Receipts and Expenditure.
68.	69.	70.	71.	
70	108	88·5	50	Average Number of Children paid for by Treasury.
–	–	·25	1	Average Number of Children under 6 years of age, and not paid for by Treasury.
·9	–	–	0·6	Average Number of Children in excess of limit, and not paid for by Treasury.
8	14	–	8	Average Number of Voluntary Inmates.
£ s. d.	£ s. d.	£ s. d.	£ s. d.	Receipts.
912 10 0	1,809 0 0	315 0 6	664 3 0	Treasury Allowances.
–	–	405 14 11	–	Subscriptions, Legacies, Donations, &c.
840 6 10	348 3 1	158 5 8	767 7 10	Payments from County or Borough Rates.
22 0 0	298 0 1	–	96 0 7	Payments for Voluntary Inmates.
–	–	–	–	Hire of Labour.
–	–	34 15 6	–	Sundries.
1,974 16 10	1,930 4 2	1,006 16 7	1,527 11 5	Total Receipts.
				Expenditure.
				Ordinary Charges.
128 0 0	136 0 0	186 0 0	265 0 0	Officers' Pay (Salaries & Wages).
–	184 0 0	–	115 0 0	Officers' Rations.
572 0 0	1,007 9 1	262 17 4	481 14 9	Food for Inmates.
168 14 9	324 3 2	89 1 11	79 18 0	Clothing of Inmates.
78 7 1	222 5 9	178 13 5	87 13 6	Washing, Fuel, and Light.
60 0 0	215 14 1	51 6 2	28 5 9	Repairs, Rates, and Taxes.
55 0 0	106 7 8	35 5 8	36 8 1	Furniture and House Sundries.
15 0 0	6 6 3	31 14 3	13 0 0	Printing and Office Expenses.
–	10 0 4	5 14 0	17 16 8	Travelling and Police Charges.
22 0 0	28 18 7	2 13 8	81 5 10	Medical Expenses, Funerals, &c.
9 6 0	75 8 1	5 12 0	11 0 11	Sundries, Rewards, &c.
1,104 1 10	2,317 9 8	853 0 6	1,125 4 8	Total Ordinary Charges.
				Extra Charges.
30 0 0	30 0 0	–	–	Rent of School Premises.
180 0 0	93 4 0	98 17 4	70 0 0	Interest.
58 9 4	54 8 0	23 14 11	–	Disposal, Home.
–	–	–	–	Disposal, Emigration.
–	–	–	–	Building and Land.
268 9 4	178 12 0	122 12 3	70 0 0	Total Extra Charges.
1,372 11 2	2,494 1 8	976 12 9	1,196 4 5	Total Expenditure.
				Industrial Department.

15.—Industrial Schools.—Summary of Accounts of Receipts

Industrial Schools.	Total Number of Children whose Maintenance is included in Expenditure.	Total Cost of Maintenance and Management.	Add Rent and Interest.
		£ s. d.	£ s. d.
1. Grumplan, ...	310·60	4,640 17 9	—
2. Balmoral, ...	318	2,101 6 6	—
3. Hampton House, ...	170	2,230 17 9	100 7 0
4. St. Patrick's, Milltown	150·7	2,093 5 9	90 0 0
5. St. Patrick's, Crumlin Road, . .	66	1,071 11 9	760 0 0
6. Sacred Heart, Abbeyville, . . .	60	1,134 8 5	100 0 0
7. Shamrock Lodge, ...	60	1,074 0 11	34 11 0
8. Middletown, ...	80	914 2 9	42 0 0
9. Lurgan, ...	40	736 2 5	100 14 5
10. St. Joseph's, Cavan, ...	64	1,300 7 6	200 0 0
11. Ennis, ...	72	1,090 3 7	291 10 0
12. St. Aloysius, Clonakilty, . . .	180·5	2,247 16 11	385 10 11
13. St. Colman's, Queenstown . . .	60	750 10 6	90 0 0
14. Our Lady of Mercy, Kinsale, . .	150	2,087 4 10	254 0 0
15. Danesfort, Upton, ...	201	3,640 17 9	187 14 6
16. Cork Protestant School, . . .	54	1,010 17 9	200 10 0
17. Mallow, ...	84	1,145 1 5	110 0 0
18. Passage West, ...	81	1,164 0 0	100 0 0
19. Baltimore, ...	143	2,182 18 10	166 7 5
20. St. Finbarr's, Cork, ...	201	3,500 5 6	87 18 6
21. Greenmount, Cork, ...	201	3,004 5 7	111 10 0
22. Training Home, ...	44·8	572 0 7	70 0 0
23. Killybegs, ...	100	1,707 0 7	67 7 6
24. Artane, ...	800	15,011 14 4	1,300 7 0
25. Booterstown, ...	60	1,040 12 10	87 17 6
26. St. Mary's, Carysfort, ...	80	1,309 15 6	50 0 0
27. Golden Bridge, ...	190	2,160 13 6½	400 0 0
28. Carriglea, ...	123	2,334 13 6	410 11 5
29. St. Mary's, Lakelands, ...	70	1,160 10 0	300 0 0
30. Meath, co. Dublin, ...	183	2,345 0 4	80 0 0
31. Merrion, ...	173	2,334 0 0	193 15 0
32. Heytesbury-street, Dublin, . .	33	410 19 10	32 0 0
33. St. Brigid's, Loughrea, . . .	110	1,734 0 0	100 0 0
34. St. Joseph's, Ballinasloe, . .	40	1,350 0 0	121 0 0
35. Clifden, ...	47·4	1,047 0 8	33 0 0
36. Letterfrack, ...	151	2,722 18 4	300 0 0
37. Oughterard, ...	40	715 1 0	40 0 0
38. St. Anne's, Galway, ...	60	1,303 5 1	100 0 0
39. Salt Hill, Galway	200	3,000 0 0	247 17 6

and Expenditure during the year ending 31st December, 1888.

Add Expenses of Disposal.			Deduct Industrial Profit.			Add Industrial Loss.			Net Cost per Head with these additions or deductions.			Industrial Schools.
£	s.	d.	£	s.	d.	£	s.	d.	£	s.	d.	
150	0	0	248	16	3	—			17	17	6	Grampian.
15	10	0	328	2	11	—			16	10	1	Balmoral.
42	0	8	328	14	6	—			14	0	8	Hampton House.
128	14	8	86	5	8	—			18	17	6	St. Patrick's, Kilkenny.
100	10	4	6	5	8	—			20	6	4	St. Patrick's, Crumlin Road.
80	0	0	35	15	0	—			20	10	7	Sacred Heart, Abbeyville.
54	19	10	201	5	8	—			13	6	2	Shamrock Lodge.
71	10	0	81	1	8	—			16	10	6	Middletown.
15	0	0	95	7	8	—			17	10	2	Lurgan.
67	6	9	100	15	4	—			17	13	6	St. Joseph's, Cavan.
16	8	4	80	16	5	—			11	7	1	Ennis.
84	10	8	170	5	0	—			15	6	7	St. Aloysius, Clonakilty.
4	18	8	78	0	0	—			18	7	6	St. Coleman's, Queenstown.
50	0	8	173	10	8	—			16	16	7	Our Lady of Mercy, Kinsale.
87	2	2	181	14	1	—			17	7	4	[illegible], Upton.
44	15	6	248	17	0	—			16	13	8	Cork Protestant School.
38	6	0	61	15	5	—			21	5	6	Mallow.
21	6	0	14	0	0	—			20	5	10	Passage West.
45	11	10	144	6	11½	—			15	4	2	Baltimore.

15.—Industrial Schools.—Summary of Accounts of Receipts and

Industrial Schools.	Total Number of Children whose Maintenance is included in Expenditure.	Total Cost of Maintenance and Management.	Add Rent and Interest.
		£ s. d.	£ s. d.
40. St. Joseph's, Killarney, . . .	103	1,[illegible] 10 [illegible]	7[illegible] 0 0
41. St. Joseph's, Tralee, . . .	160	2,279 10 7	—
42. Pembroke Alms House, Tralee, .	70	1,[illegible] 10 0	—
43. Kilkenny, Boys, ...	174	2,910 1 1½	274 0 0
44. Do. Girls, ...	100	2,[illegible] 14 11	731 10 0
45. St. John's, Parsonstown, . . .	78·1	1,[illegible] 7 6½	78 11 10
46. St. George's, Limerick, . .	113	1,[illegible] 0 10	3[illegible] 0 0
47. St. Vincent's, Limerick, . . .	130	2,049 0 0	[illegible] 0 0
48. Limerick, Boys, ...	[illegible]	2,104 17 6	[illegible] 7 0
49. Our Lady of Benmore, Newtownforbes,	164	6,287 7 6½	20 0 0
50. House of Charity, Drogheda, . .	97	1,[illegible] 4 6	44 0 0
51. Dundalk, ...	60	1,094 16 9	22 13 0
52. St. Columba, Westport, . . .	102	1,046 7 6	215 0 0
53. Ballaghaderreen, ...	76	1,492 10 6	[illegible] 0 0
54. St. Martha's, Monaghan, . . .	75	1,379 9 10	15 0 0
55. St. Monica's, Roscommon, . . .	13	1,277 12 11	60 0 0
56. Summerhill, Athlone, . . .	176	3,[illegible] 14 11	167 10 0
57. Banada Abbey, Tubbercurry, . .	[illegible]	1,010 5 5	75 10 6
58. St. Laurence, Sligo, ...	143	2,040 7 4	[illegible] 15 0
59. Clonmel, ...	100·7	2,010 2 4½	102 15 4
60. St. Augustine's, Templemore. . .	61	1,061 19 7	100 0 0
61. St. Francis, Cashel, ...	10[illegible]	1,[illegible] 0 0	25 10 3
62. St. Louis, Thurles, ...	45	610 10 0	15 0 0
63. Tipperary, ...	54	1,[illegible] 11 11	[illegible] 14 5
64. St. Catherine's, Strabane . . .	30	1,077 16 4	142 10 0
65. Cappoquin, ...	54	870 17 1	70 0 0
66. St. Dominick, Waterford, . . .	165	2,[illegible] 10 11	7[illegible] 0 0
67. Mount Carmel, Moate, . . .	50·2	640 0 7	131 0 0
68. St. Aidan's, New Ross, . . .	77	1,[illegible] 1 10	210 0 0
69. St. Michael's, Wexford, . . .	119	2,317 0 0	102 4 0
70. Meath, Bray, ...	20·3	[illegible] 0 0	60 17 4
71. St. Kyran's, Rathdrum . . .	63·5	1,170 4 4	70 0 0

EXPENDITURE during the year ending 31st December, 1898—*continued.*

Add Expenses of Disposal.	Deduct Industrial Profit.	Add Industrial Loss.	Net Cost per Head with these additions or deductions.	INDUSTRIAL SCHOOLS.
£ s. d.	£ s. d.	£ s. d.	£ s. d.	
44 0 0	63 14 0	—	15 10 0	St. Joseph's, Killarney.
40 15 11	148 3 0	—	21 5 7	St. Joseph's, Tralee.
41 0 0	80 0 4	—	14 15 0	Pembroke Alms House, Tralee.
—	150 10 0	—	15 3 1	Kilkenny Boys.
60 0 0	268 8 4	—	20 0 3	Do. Girls.
34 15 8	118 0 6	—	17 14 7	St. John's, Parsonstown.
65 15 9	83 11 1	—	18 0 1	St. George's, Limerick.
114 0 8	163 8 10½	—	23 1 6	St. Vincent's, Limerick.
39 19 6	277 18 0	—	16 15 4	Limerick, Boys.
101 18 9	818 0 11½	—	19 3 4	Our Lady of Succour, Newtownforbes.
..	16 5 5	—	19 9 1	House of Charity, Drogheda.
88 10 0	564 19 0	—	17 7 8	Dundalk.
67 14 0	71 16 0	—	15 10 11	St. Columba, Westport.
15 0 0	98 16 10	—	20 15 6	Ballaghaderreen.
39 4 0	83 1 10	—	18 1 1	St. Martha's, Monaghan.
—	—	87 8 5	19 2 1	St. Monica's, Roscommon.
—	919 14 8	—	18 15 9	Summerhill, Athlone.
—	116 19 3	—	19 11 11	Benada Abbey, Tubbercurry.
27 15 0	286 11 1	—	16 11 6	St. Laurence, Sligo.
65 16 1	366 18 6	—	14 14 3	Clonmel.
—	168 13 8	—	17 13 0	St. Augustine's, Templemore.
48 3 9	147 8 6	—	17 6 6	St. Francis, Cashel.
34 10 6	48 10 11	—	15 4 8	St. Louis, Thurles.
96 10 11	457 14 5	—	16 0 8	Tipperary.
68 0 0	63 11 6	—	16 0 7	St. Catherine's, Strabane.

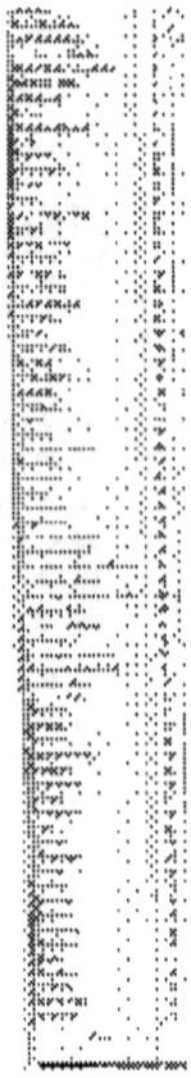

16.—Return giving (1st), the Population of each County and Town in Ireland as taken at Census, 1891; (2nd), the Amount paid by each County for Support of Children in Reformatory Schools during the past year (1898); (3rd), the Number of Children under Detention in Reformatory Schools from each County on 31st December, 1898.

Counties and Towns.	Population.	Amount contributed in 1898.	No. of Children under Detention in Reformatory Schools from each County on 31st Dec., 1898.
		£ s. d.	
Antrim,*	[illegible]	[illegible]	[illegible]
Armagh,	[illegible]	[illegible]	3
Carlow,	[illegible]	[illegible]	[illegible]
Cavan,	[illegible]	[illegible]	[illegible]
Clare,	[illegible]	[illegible]	[illegible]
Cork,	[illegible]	[illegible]	[illegible]
Cork City,	[illegible]	[illegible]	[illegible]
Donegal,	[illegible]	[illegible]	[illegible]
Down,	[illegible]	[illegible]	[illegible]
Dublin,	[illegible]	[illegible]	[illegible]
Dublin City,	[illegible]	[illegible]	[illegible]
Fermanagh,	[illegible]	[illegible]	[illegible]
Galway,	[illegible]	[illegible]	[illegible]
Galway Town,	[illegible]	[illegible]	[illegible]
Kerry,	[illegible]	[illegible]	18
Kildare,	[illegible]	[illegible]	[illegible]
Kilkenny,	[illegible]	1 1 2	–
Kilkenny City,	[illegible]	[illegible]	[illegible]
King's,	[illegible]	[illegible]	[illegible]
Leitrim,	[illegible]	[illegible]	–
Limerick,	[illegible]	[illegible]	[illegible]
Limerick City,	[illegible]	[illegible]	[illegible]
Londonderry,	[illegible]	[illegible]	[illegible]
Longford,	[illegible]	[illegible]	[illegible]
Louth,	[illegible]	[illegible]	[illegible]
Drogheda Town,	[illegible]	[illegible]	[illegible]
Mayo,	[illegible]	[illegible]	[illegible]
Meath,	[illegible]	[illegible]	[illegible]
Monaghan,	[illegible]	[illegible]	–
Queen's,	[illegible]	[illegible]	[illegible]
Roscommon,	[illegible]	[illegible]	[illegible]
Sligo,	[illegible]	[illegible]	[illegible]
Tipperary, N.R.,	[illegible]	[illegible]	1
Tipperary, S.R.,	[illegible]	[illegible]	13
Tyrone,	[illegible]	[illegible]	[illegible]
Waterford,	[illegible]	[illegible]	[illegible]
Waterford City,	[illegible]	[illegible]	[illegible]
Westmeath,	[illegible]	[illegible]	[illegible]
Wexford,	[illegible]	[illegible]	–
Wicklow,	[illegible]	[illegible]	[illegible]
Total,	[illegible]	[illegible]	[illegible]

* All the children chargeable to the city of Belfast are included in the county Antrim figures.

19.—Return giving (1st), the Population of each County and Town in Ireland as taken at Census, 1891; (2nd), the amount paid by each County for Support of Children in Industrial Schools during the past year (1898); (3rd), the Number of Children under Detention in Industrial Schools from each County on 31st December, 1898.

Counties and Towns.	Population.	Amount contributed in 1898.	No. of Children under Detention in Industrial Schools from each County on 31st Dec., 1898.
		£ s. d.	
Antrim,	428,128	2,424 12 11	1,337*
Armagh,	143,289	285 4 8	24
Carlow,	40,936	—	7
Cavan,	111,917	—	60
Clare,	124,483	472 1 0	128
Cork,	[illegible]	4,218 9 1	294
Cork City,	75,345	1,308 5 9	277
Donegal,	185,635	287 4 0	59
Down,	267,059	122 11 10	40
Dublin,	174,215	5,209 3 4	682
Dublin City,	245,001	12,152 16 3	2,042
Fermanagh,	74,170	162 7 11	92
Galway,	197,233	3,088 16 8	432
Galway Town,	16,959	612 11 8	126
Kerry,	179,136	843 2 4	213
Kildare,	70,206	888 3 11	69
Kilkenny,	76,813	878 3 6	167
Kilkenny City,	11,048	288 17 1	84
King's,	65,563	183 14 8	22
Leitrim,	78,618	130 10 9	32
Limerick,	121,764	642 8 10	131
Limerick City,	37,155	588 10 11	164
Londonderry,	148,069	222 10 1	40
Longford,	52,647	888 3 7	41
Louth,	61,105	403 10 9	60
Drogheda Town,	11,873	876 13 1	51
Mayo,	219,034	1,218 8 3	268
Meath,	76,987	147 11 11	46
Monaghan,	86,206	180 16 8	39
Queen's,	64,883	—	15
Roscommon,	114,397	966 10 8	137
Sligo,	98,013	626 16 0	121
Tipperary, N. R.,	71,280	189 11 6	80
Tipperary, S. R.,	91,638	136 2 3	67
Tyrone,	171,401	542 5 1	106
Waterford,	77,308	77 4 11	38
Waterford City,	20,852	684 18 0	180
Westmeath,	65,109	432 11 1	47
Wexford,	111,778	321 16 6	143
Wicklow,	62,136	225 3 4	61
Total,	4,704,750	41,391 0 8	8,715

* All the children chargeable to the city of Belfast are included in the county Antrim figures.

20.—Return showing the Rates paid by each County per Head per Week for Children in Industrial and Reformatory Schools during the Year ending 31st of December, 1898.

Grand Jury or Town Council.	Rates.		Observations.
	To Reformatories.	To Industrial Schools.	
Co. Antrim,	[illegible]	[illegible] and 2s.	3s. to [illegible] boys; 2s. 6d. to all others.
" Armagh,	[illegible]	[illegible]	[illegible] for boys; 1s. 6d. for girls.
" Carlow,	[illegible]	Nil.	—
" Cavan,	[illegible]	Nil.	—
" Clare,	[illegible]	2s.	—
" Cork,	[illegible]	2s.	—
City of Cork (Corporation).	[illegible]	2s., 1s. 6d., and 1s.	2s. and 1s. 6d. for boys. 1s. 6d. and 1s. for girls in Cork schools; and 1s. for girls in schools outside the city.
Co. Donegal,	[illegible]	[illegible]	[illegible] for children in the Lurgan, Drogheda, Sligo, [illegible], and Killybegs Schools; 2s. for children in the [illegible], Baltimore, [illegible] and [illegible] Schools; 1s. 6d. for children in [illegible] School.
" Down,	[illegible]	[illegible]	—
" Dublin,	[illegible]	[illegible]	—
City of Dublin,	[illegible] and 3s.	2s.	2s. 6d. to Glencree Reformatory; 2s. to all others.
Co. Fermanagh,	[illegible]	[illegible] and 2s.	2s. to the Cavan and [illegible] Schools; 1s. 6d. to all others.
" Galway,	[illegible]	2s.	—
Town of Galway,	[illegible]	2s.	—
Co. Kerry,	[illegible]	2s. and 1s.	2s. for boys; 1s. for girls.
" Kildare,	[illegible]	[illegible]	—
" Kilkenny,	[illegible]	[illegible]	—
City of Kilkenny,	[illegible]	[illegible], and 1s. 6d.	[illegible] to Artane; 2s. to [illegible] School; 1s. 6d. to the [illegible] and Kilkenny (Female) Schools.
King's Co.,	[illegible]	[illegible] and 2s.	[illegible] to Artane; 2s. to all others.
Co. Leitrim,	[illegible]	[illegible] and 2s.	2s. to Cavan School; 1s. 6d. to all others.
" Limerick,	[illegible]	2s.	—
City of Limerick,	[illegible] and 2s.	2s.	2s. 6d. for boys and 2s. for girls.

20.—Return showing the Rates paid by each County—*continued.*

Grand Jury or Town Council.	Rates: To Reformatories.	Rates: To Industrial Schools.	Observations.
Co. Londonderry,	2s. 6d. and 3s.	[illegible] and 3s.	[illegible] for boys, and 2s. for girls.
„ Longford,	2s. 6d.	3s. 6d., 3s., and 1s. 6d.	[illegible]
„ Louth,	3s. 6d.	2s. 6d. and 3s.	[illegible]
Town of Drogheda,	2s. 6d. and 3s.	3s. 6d. and 3s.	3s. 6d. for boys and 2s. for girls.
Co. Mayo,	3s. 6d.	3s.	—
„ Meath,	2s. 6d.	3s. 6d. and 3s.	2s. to Kilkenny (Male); 3s. 6d. to all others.
„ Monaghan,	2s. 6d.	3s. 6d. and 3s.	3s. to Cavan School; 3s. 6d. to all others.
Queen's Co.,	2s.	Nil.	—
Co. Roscommon,	2s. 6d. and 3s.	3s.	[illegible]
„ Sligo,	2s. 6d.	3s. 6d.	—
„ Tipperary, N.R.,	2s. 6d.	3s.	—
„ Tipperary, S.R.,	2s. 6d.	2s. 6d.	—
„ Tyrone,	2s. 6d.	2s. 6d. and 3s.	3s. to Strabane School; 2s. 6d. to all others.
„ Waterford,	2s. 6d.	2s.	The Co. Waterford Grand Jury paid only for children in Philipstown Reformatory and Kilkenny Industrial School.
City of Waterford,	2s. 6d.	3s. 6d. and 2s.	2s. 6d. to children in the Artane, [illegible], Cappoquin, and Clonmel Schools; 2s. to Kilkenny (Female), [illegible], and Waterford Schools.
Co. Westmeath,	2s. 6d. and 3s.	3s. 6d.	3s. to Philipstown; 2s. 6d. to all others.
„ Wexford,	2s. 6d.	3s. 6d., 3s., 2s. 6d., and 2s.	3s. 6d. to the Artane, Cappoquin, Letterfrack, Clonmel, Limerick (Male), and [illegible] Schools; 3s. to [illegible]; 2s. 6d. and 2s. to the Wexford, New Ross, Bray, and Kilkenny (Male) Schools; 2s. to Waterford School.
„ Wicklow,	3s.	3s.	—

31.—Showing the Causes of Deaths of Children under Detention in year ending the 31st

Schools	Lung Disease.		Brain Disease.		Heart Disease.		Mesenteric and Bowel Disease.		Fever.	
	M.	F.	M.	F.	M.	F.	M.	F.	M.	F.
Reformatory.										
High Park, Dublin,	-	1	-	-	-	-	-	-	-	-
St. Conleth's, Philipstown,	1	-	-	-	-	-	-	-	-	-
Total,	1	1	-	-	-	-	-	-	-	-
Industrial Schools.										
Grampian,	3	-	2	-	-	-	-	-	-	-
Hampton House,	-	-	-	-	-	-	-	-	-	-
St. Patrick's (Male),	-	-	-	-	-	-	1	-	-	-
St. Patrick's (Female),	-	1	-	1	-	-	-	-	-	-
Abbeyville,	-	1	-	-	-	-	-	-	-	-
Shamrock Lodge,	-	1	-	-	-	-	-	-	-	-
Middletown,	-	1	-	1	-	-	-	-	-	-
Ennis,	-	2	-	-	-	-	-	-	-	-
St. Aloysius, Clonakilty,	-	1	-	-	-	-	-	-	-	-
Kinsale,	-	1	-	-	-	-	-	-	-	-
Danesfort, Upton,	1	-	-	-	-	-	-	-	-	-
Mallow,	-	3	-	1	-	-	-	-	-	-
St. Finbar's,	-	-	-	-	-	-	-	-	-	-
Greenmount,	1	-	-	-	-	-	-	-	-	-
Artane,	1	-	-	-	1	-	-	-	-	-
Baxterstown,	-	-	-	2	-	-	-	-	-	-
Golden Bridge,	-	-	-	1	-	1	-	-	-	-
Lakelands,	-	-	-	-	-	-	-	-	-	-
Merrion, Blackrock,	-	-	-	-	-	-	1	-	-	-
Clifden,	-	1	-	-	-	-	-	-	-	-
Letterfrack,	-	-	-	-	-	-	-	-	-	-
Oughterard,	-	-	-	-	-	1	-	-	-	-
St. Anne's, Galway,	-	1	-	-	-	-	-	-	-	-
Killarney,	-	-	-	-	-	-	-	1	-	-
Pembroke Alms House, Tralee,	-	1	-	-	-	-	-	-	-	-
Kilkenny (Male),	3	-	-	-	-	-	-	-	-	-
Do. (Female),	-	1	-	-	-	-	-	-	-	-
St. George's, Limerick,	-	2	-	-	-	1	-	-	-	-
St. Vincent's, do.,	-	3	-	-	-	-	-	-	-	-
Limerick (Male),	1	-	-	-	-	-	-	-	-	-
Newtownforbes,	-	-	-	-	-	-	-	-	-	1
Drogheda,	1	-	-	-	-	-	-	-	-	-
Dundalk,	-	-	-	-	-	-	-	-	-	-
St. Monica's, Roscommon,	-	-	-	-	-	-	-	-	-	-
Summer Hill,	-	-	-	-	-	-	-	-	-	-
Benada Abbey,	-	1	-	-	-	-	-	-	-	-
Clonmel,	-	-	-	-	1	-	-	-	-	-
Templemore,	-	2	-	-	-	-	-	-	-	-
St. Dominick's, Waterford,	-	2	-	-	-	1	-	-	-	-
Mount Carmel, Moate,	-	1	-	1	-	-	-	-	-	-
St. Michael's, Wexford,	-	1	-	1	-	-	-	-	-	-
Total,	10	28	2	8	2	4	2	1	-	1

Reformatory and Industrial Schools, and on Licence, during the of December, 1898.

Accidental Deaths.		Spinal and Hip Disease.		Other Causes.		Total.			Schools.
M.	F.	M.	F.	M.	F.	Male.	Female.	Total.	
									Reformatory.
-	-	-	-	-	-	-	1	1	High Park, Dublin.
-	-	-	-	-	-	1	-	1	St. Conleth's, Philipstown.
-	-	-	-	-	-	1	1	2	
									Industrial Schools.
-	-	-	-	-	-	5	-	5	Orampion.
-	1	-	-	-	-	-	1	1	Hampton House.
-	-	-	-	-	-	1	-	1	St. Patrick's (Male).
-	-	-	-	-	-	-	2	2	St. Patrick's (Female).
-	-	-	-	-	-	-	1	1	Abbeyville.
-	-	-	-	-	-	-	1	1	Shamrock Lodge.
-	-	-	-	-	-	-	3	3	Middletown.
-	-	-	-	-	-	-	2	2	Ennis.
-	-	-	-	-	-	-	1	1	St. Aloysius, Clonakilty.
-	-	-	-	-	-	-	1	1	Kinsale.
-	-	-	-	-	-	1	-	1	Danesfort, Upton.
-	-	-	-	-	-	-	3	3	Mallow.
-	-	-	-	-	2	-	3	3	St. Finbar's.
-	-	-	-	-	-	1	-	1	Greenmount.
-	-	-	-	-	-	3	-	3	Artane.
-	-	-	-	-	-	-	2	2	Booterstown.
-	-	-	-	-	-	-	3	3	Golden Bridge.
-	-	-	-	-	1	-	1	1	Lakelands.
-	-	-	-	-	-	1	-	1	Meath, Blackrock.
-	-	-	-	-	-	-	1	1	Clifden.
-	-	-	-	1	-	1	-	1	Letterfrack.
-	-	-	-	-	-	-	1	1	Oughterard.
-	-	-	-	-	-	-	1	1	St. Anne's, Galway.
-	-	-	-	-	-	-	1	1	Killarney.
-	-	-	-	-	-	-	1	1	Pembroke Alms House, Tralee.
-	-	-	-	-	-	2	-	2	Kilkenny (Male).
-	-	-	-	-	-	-	1	1	Do. (Female).
-	-	-	-	-	1	-	4	4	St. George's, Limerick.
-	-	-	-	-	-	-	6	6	St. Vincent's, do.
-	-	-	-	-	-	1	-	1	Limerick (Male).
-	-	-	-	-	-	-	1	1	Newtownforbes.
-	-	-	-	-	-	1	-	1	Drogheda.
-	-	-	1	-	-	-	1	1	Dundalk.
-	-	-	-	-	1	-	1	1	St. Monica's, Roscommon.
-	-	-	-	-	2	-	2	2	Summer Hill.
-	-	-	-	-	-	-	1	1	Benada Abbey.
-	-	-	-	-	-	1	-	1	Clonmel.
-	-	-	-	-	-	-	3	3	Templemore.
-	-	-	-	-	-	-	3	3	St. Dominick, Waterford.
-	-	-	1	-	-	-	3	3	Mount Carmel, Moate.
-	-	-	1	-	-	-	3	3	St. Michael's, Wexford.
-	1	-	3	1	7	17	41	58	Total.

22.—Return—Showing the Causes for which Children were Committed

Schools.	A child found begging or receiving alms, whether doing so actually or under pretext of selling anything or offering anything for sale. 1.		A child being in any street or public place for the purpose of begging or receiving alms, whether actually doing so or under pretext of selling anything or offering anything for sale. 2.		A child found wandering and not having any home. 3.		A child found wandering, and not having any settled place of abode. 4.		A child found wandering, and not having proper guardianship. 5.	
	M.	F.	M.	F.	M.	F.	M.	F.	M.	F.
Glencree,	[illegible]	[illegible]	[illegible]	[illegible]	[illegible]	[illegible]	[illegible]	[illegible]	[illegible]	[illegible]
[illegible]	[illegible]	[illegible]	[illegible]	[illegible]	[illegible]	[illegible]	[illegible]	[illegible]	[illegible]	[illegible]
[illegible]	[illegible]	[illegible]	[illegible]	[illegible]	[illegible]	[illegible]	[illegible]	[illegible]	[illegible]	[illegible]
St. Patrick's (Male),	[illegible]	[illegible]	[illegible]	[illegible]	[illegible]	[illegible]	[illegible]	[illegible]	[illegible]	[illegible]
Do. (Female),	[illegible]	[illegible]	[illegible]	[illegible]	[illegible]	[illegible]	[illegible]	[illegible]	[illegible]	[illegible]
[illegible]	[illegible]	[illegible]	[illegible]	[illegible]	[illegible]	[illegible]	[illegible]	[illegible]	[illegible]	[illegible]
[illegible] Lodge,	[illegible]	[illegible]	[illegible]	[illegible]	[illegible]	[illegible]	[illegible]	[illegible]	[illegible]	[illegible]
[illegible]	[illegible]	[illegible]	[illegible]	[illegible]	[illegible]	[illegible]	[illegible]	[illegible]	[illegible]	[illegible]
[illegible]	[illegible]	[illegible]	[illegible]	[illegible]	[illegible]	[illegible]	[illegible]	[illegible]	[illegible]	[illegible]
[illegible]	[illegible]	[illegible]	[illegible]	[illegible]	[illegible]	[illegible]	[illegible]	[illegible]	[illegible]	[illegible]
[illegible]	[illegible]	[illegible]	[illegible]	[illegible]	[illegible]	[illegible]	[illegible]	[illegible]	[illegible]	[illegible]
[illegible]	[illegible]	[illegible]	[illegible]	[illegible]	[illegible]	[illegible]	[illegible]	[illegible]	[illegible]	[illegible]
Queenstown,	[illegible]	[illegible]	[illegible]	[illegible]	[illegible]	[illegible]	[illegible]	[illegible]	[illegible]	[illegible]
Kinsale,	[illegible]	[illegible]	[illegible]	[illegible]	[illegible]	[illegible]	[illegible]	[illegible]	[illegible]	[illegible]
[illegible]	[illegible]	[illegible]	[illegible]	[illegible]	[illegible]	[illegible]	[illegible]	[illegible]	[illegible]	[illegible]
Cork Protestant,	[illegible]	[illegible]	[illegible]	[illegible]	[illegible]	[illegible]	[illegible]	[illegible]	[illegible]	[illegible]
Mallow,	[illegible]	[illegible]	[illegible]	[illegible]	[illegible]	[illegible]	[illegible]	[illegible]	[illegible]	[illegible]
Passage West,	[illegible]	[illegible]	[illegible]	[illegible]	[illegible]	[illegible]	[illegible]	[illegible]	[illegible]	[illegible]
Baltimore,	[illegible]	[illegible]	[illegible]	[illegible]	[illegible]	[illegible]	[illegible]	[illegible]	[illegible]	[illegible]
St. Finbar's,	[illegible]	[illegible]	[illegible]	[illegible]	[illegible]	[illegible]	[illegible]	[illegible]	[illegible]	[illegible]
Greenmount,	[illegible]	[illegible]	[illegible]	[illegible]	[illegible]	[illegible]	[illegible]	[illegible]	[illegible]	[illegible]
Training Home,	[illegible]	[illegible]	[illegible]	[illegible]	[illegible]	[illegible]	[illegible]	[illegible]	[illegible]	[illegible]
[illegible]	[illegible]	[illegible]	[illegible]	[illegible]	[illegible]	[illegible]	[illegible]	[illegible]	[illegible]	[illegible]
Artane,	[illegible]	[illegible]	[illegible]	[illegible]	[illegible]	[illegible]	[illegible]	[illegible]	[illegible]	[illegible]
[illegible]	[illegible]	[illegible]	[illegible]	[illegible]	[illegible]	[illegible]	[illegible]	[illegible]	[illegible]	[illegible]
[illegible]	[illegible]	[illegible]	[illegible]	[illegible]	[illegible]	[illegible]	[illegible]	[illegible]	[illegible]	[illegible]
Golden Bridge,	[illegible]	[illegible]	[illegible]	[illegible]	[illegible]	[illegible]	[illegible]	[illegible]	[illegible]	[illegible]
Carriglea Park,	[illegible]	[illegible]	[illegible]	[illegible]	[illegible]	[illegible]	[illegible]	[illegible]	[illegible]	[illegible]
[illegible]	[illegible]	[illegible]	[illegible]	[illegible]	[illegible]	[illegible]	[illegible]	[illegible]	[illegible]	[illegible]
[illegible], Blackrock,	[illegible]	[illegible]	[illegible]	[illegible]	[illegible]	[illegible]	[illegible]	[illegible]	[illegible]	[illegible]
[illegible]	[illegible]	[illegible]	[illegible]	[illegible]	[illegible]	[illegible]	[illegible]	[illegible]	[illegible]	[illegible]
[illegible]-street,	[illegible]	[illegible]	[illegible]	[illegible]	[illegible]	[illegible]	[illegible]	[illegible]	[illegible]	[illegible]
[illegible]	[illegible]	[illegible]	[illegible]	[illegible]	[illegible]	[illegible]	[illegible]	[illegible]	[illegible]	[illegible]
Ballinasloe,	[illegible]	[illegible]	[illegible]	[illegible]	[illegible]	[illegible]	[illegible]	[illegible]	[illegible]	[illegible]
Clifden,	[illegible]	[illegible]	[illegible]	[illegible]	[illegible]	[illegible]	[illegible]	[illegible]	[illegible]	[illegible]
Letterfrack,	[illegible]	[illegible]	[illegible]	[illegible]	[illegible]	[illegible]	[illegible]	[illegible]	[illegible]	[illegible]
Oughterard,	[illegible]	[illegible]	[illegible]	[illegible]	[illegible]	[illegible]	[illegible]	[illegible]	[illegible]	[illegible]
St. Anne's, Galway,	[illegible]	[illegible]	[illegible]	[illegible]	[illegible]	[illegible]	[illegible]	[illegible]	[illegible]	[illegible]
Salt Hill, Galway,	[illegible]	[illegible]	[illegible]	[illegible]	[illegible]	[illegible]	[illegible]	[illegible]	[illegible]	[illegible]
Killarney,	[illegible]	[illegible]	[illegible]	[illegible]	[illegible]	[illegible]	[illegible]	[illegible]	[illegible]	[illegible]
St. Joseph's, Tralee,	[illegible]	[illegible]	[illegible]	[illegible]	[illegible]	[illegible]	[illegible]	[illegible]	[illegible]	[illegible]
Pembroke Alms House, Tralee,	[illegible]	[illegible]	[illegible]	[illegible]	[illegible]	[illegible]	[illegible]	[illegible]	[illegible]	[illegible]
Kilkenny (Male),	[illegible]	[illegible]	[illegible]	[illegible]	[illegible]	[illegible]	[illegible]	[illegible]	[illegible]	[illegible]
Do. (Female),	[illegible]	[illegible]	[illegible]	[illegible]	[illegible]	[illegible]	[illegible]	[illegible]	[illegible]	[illegible]
[illegible]	[illegible]	[illegible]	[illegible]	[illegible]	[illegible]	[illegible]	[illegible]	[illegible]	[illegible]	[illegible]
St. George's, Limerick,	[illegible]	[illegible]	[illegible]	[illegible]	[illegible]	[illegible]	[illegible]	[illegible]	[illegible]	[illegible]
St. Vincent's, Limerick,	[illegible]	[illegible]	[illegible]	[illegible]	[illegible]	[illegible]	[illegible]	[illegible]	[illegible]	[illegible]
Limerick (Male),	[illegible]	[illegible]	[illegible]	[illegible]	[illegible]	[illegible]	[illegible]	[illegible]	[illegible]	[illegible]
Newtownforbes,	[illegible]	[illegible]	[illegible]	[illegible]	[illegible]	[illegible]	[illegible]	[illegible]	[illegible]	[illegible]
[illegible]	[illegible]	[illegible]	[illegible]	[illegible]	[illegible]	[illegible]	[illegible]	[illegible]	[illegible]	[illegible]
Dundalk,	[illegible]	[illegible]	[illegible]	[illegible]	[illegible]	[illegible]	[illegible]	[illegible]	[illegible]	[illegible]
Westport,	[illegible]	[illegible]	[illegible]	[illegible]	[illegible]	[illegible]	[illegible]	[illegible]	[illegible]	[illegible]
Ballaghaderreen,	[illegible]	[illegible]	[illegible]	[illegible]	[illegible]	[illegible]	[illegible]	[illegible]	[illegible]	[illegible]
[illegible]	[illegible]	[illegible]	[illegible]	[illegible]	[illegible]	[illegible]	[illegible]	[illegible]	[illegible]	[illegible]
[illegible]	[illegible]	[illegible]	[illegible]	[illegible]	[illegible]	[illegible]	[illegible]	[illegible]	[illegible]	[illegible]
[illegible], Athlone,	[illegible]	[illegible]	[illegible]	[illegible]	[illegible]	[illegible]	[illegible]	[illegible]	[illegible]	[illegible]
[illegible] Abbey,	[illegible]	[illegible]	[illegible]	[illegible]	[illegible]	[illegible]	[illegible]	[illegible]	[illegible]	[illegible]
Sligo,	[illegible]	[illegible]	[illegible]	[illegible]	[illegible]	[illegible]	[illegible]	[illegible]	[illegible]	[illegible]
Clonmel,	[illegible]	[illegible]	[illegible]	[illegible]	[illegible]	[illegible]	[illegible]	[illegible]	[illegible]	[illegible]
[illegible]	[illegible]	[illegible]	[illegible]	[illegible]	[illegible]	[illegible]	[illegible]	[illegible]	[illegible]	[illegible]
Cashel,	[illegible]	[illegible]	[illegible]	[illegible]	[illegible]	[illegible]	[illegible]	[illegible]	[illegible]	[illegible]
Thurles,	[illegible]	[illegible]	[illegible]	[illegible]	[illegible]	[illegible]	[illegible]	[illegible]	[illegible]	[illegible]
Tipperary,	[illegible]	[illegible]	[illegible]	[illegible]	[illegible]	[illegible]	[illegible]	[illegible]	[illegible]	[illegible]
[illegible]	[illegible]	[illegible]	[illegible]	[illegible]	[illegible]	[illegible]	[illegible]	[illegible]	[illegible]	[illegible]
Cappoquin,	[illegible]	[illegible]	[illegible]	[illegible]	[illegible]	[illegible]	[illegible]	[illegible]	[illegible]	[illegible]
St. Dominick's,	[illegible]	[illegible]	[illegible]	[illegible]	[illegible]	[illegible]	[illegible]	[illegible]	[illegible]	[illegible]
Moate,	[illegible]	[illegible]	[illegible]	[illegible]	[illegible]	[illegible]	[illegible]	[illegible]	[illegible]	[illegible]
New Ross,	[illegible]	[illegible]	[illegible]	[illegible]	[illegible]	[illegible]	[illegible]	[illegible]	[illegible]	[illegible]
Wexford,	[illegible]	[illegible]	[illegible]	[illegible]	[illegible]	[illegible]	[illegible]	[illegible]	[illegible]	[illegible]
Bray,	[illegible]	[illegible]	[illegible]	[illegible]	[illegible]	[illegible]	[illegible]	[illegible]	[illegible]	[illegible]

to Industrial Schools during the year ending 31st of December, 1898.

A child found wandering, and not having visible means of subsistence. 6.		A child found destitute, and being an orphan without any parent. 7.		A child found destitute, and having a surviving parent who is undergoing penal servitude or imprisonment. 8.		A child who frequents the company of reputed thieves. 9.		Other Causes. 10.		Total.		Observations.
M.	F.	M.	F.	M.	F.	M.	F.	M.	F.	M.	F.	
[illegible]	[illegible]	[illegible]	[illegible]	[illegible]	[illegible]	[illegible]	[illegible]	[illegible]	[illegible]	[illegible]	[illegible]	
93	26	100	101	27	49	17	6	26	1	[illegible]	[illegible]	

13.—Return of Outstanding Loans made to Reformatory and Industrial Schools.

[illegible]	[illegible]			Date of Loan.	[illegible]				[illegible]			[illegible]	Observations.
	£	s.	d.			£	s.	d.	£	s.	d.		
[illegible]	[illegible]	[illegible]	[illegible]	[illegible]	(a)	[illegible]	[illegible]	[illegible]	[illegible]	[illegible]	[illegible]	[illegible]	
[illegible] Industrial School.	[illegible]	[illegible]	[illegible]	[illegible]	(a)	[illegible]	[illegible]	[illegible]	[illegible]	[illegible]	[illegible]	[illegible]	
St. Joseph's (co. Louth)	[illegible]	[illegible]	[illegible]	[illegible]	(a)	[illegible]	[illegible]	[illegible]	[illegible]	[illegible]	[illegible]	[illegible]	
[illegible] do.	[illegible]	[illegible]	[illegible]	[illegible]	(b)	[illegible]	[illegible]	[illegible]	[illegible]	[illegible]	7	[illegible]	
St. Patrick's ([illegible]) do.	[illegible]	[illegible]	[illegible]	[illegible]	(a)	[illegible]	[illegible]	[illegible]	[illegible]	[illegible]	[illegible]	[illegible]	(a) Annuity: charge [illegible] the same throughout the [illegible].
[illegible] do.	[illegible]	[illegible]	[illegible]	[illegible]	(a)	[illegible]	[illegible]	[illegible]	[illegible]	[illegible]	[illegible]	[illegible]	(b) Repayable by equal instalments of principal with [illegible] interest charge. [illegible]
[illegible] do.	[illegible]	[illegible]	[illegible]	[illegible] June, [illegible]	(b)	[illegible]	[illegible]	[illegible]	[illegible]	[illegible]	[illegible]	1st May, [illegible]	
[illegible] do.	[illegible]	[illegible]	[illegible]	[illegible]	(a)	[illegible]	[illegible]	[illegible]	[illegible]	[illegible]	[illegible]	[illegible] May, [illegible]	
[illegible] do.	[illegible]	[illegible]	[illegible]	[illegible]	(a)	[illegible]	[illegible]	[illegible]	[illegible]	[illegible]	[illegible]	[illegible] May, [illegible]	
St. [illegible] do.	[illegible]	[illegible]	[illegible]	[illegible]	(b)	[illegible]	[illegible]	[illegible]	[illegible]	[illegible]	[illegible]	[illegible] May, [illegible]	
[illegible] do.	[illegible]	[illegible]	[illegible]	[illegible]	(a)	[illegible]	[illegible]	[illegible]	[illegible]	[illegible]	[illegible]	[illegible] May, [illegible]	

[illegible]

No. 15,879

DUBLIN CASTLE,

7th September, 1899.

SIR,

I have to acknowledge the receipt of your letter of the 2nd instant, forwarding, for submission to His Excellency the Lord Lieutenant, the Thirty-seventh Report of the Inspector of Reformatory and Industrial Schools in Ireland for the year 1898.

I am

Sir,

Your obedient Servant,

J. B. DOUGHERTY.

The Inspector of Reformatory
and Industrial Schools

www.ingramcontent.com/pod-product-compliance
Lightning Source LLC
Chambersburg PA
CBHW021523270326
41930CB00008B/1060
* 9 7 8 3 7 4 1 1 9 7 2 2 2 *